KNUFFLE P26-27
8/23/03 Mo

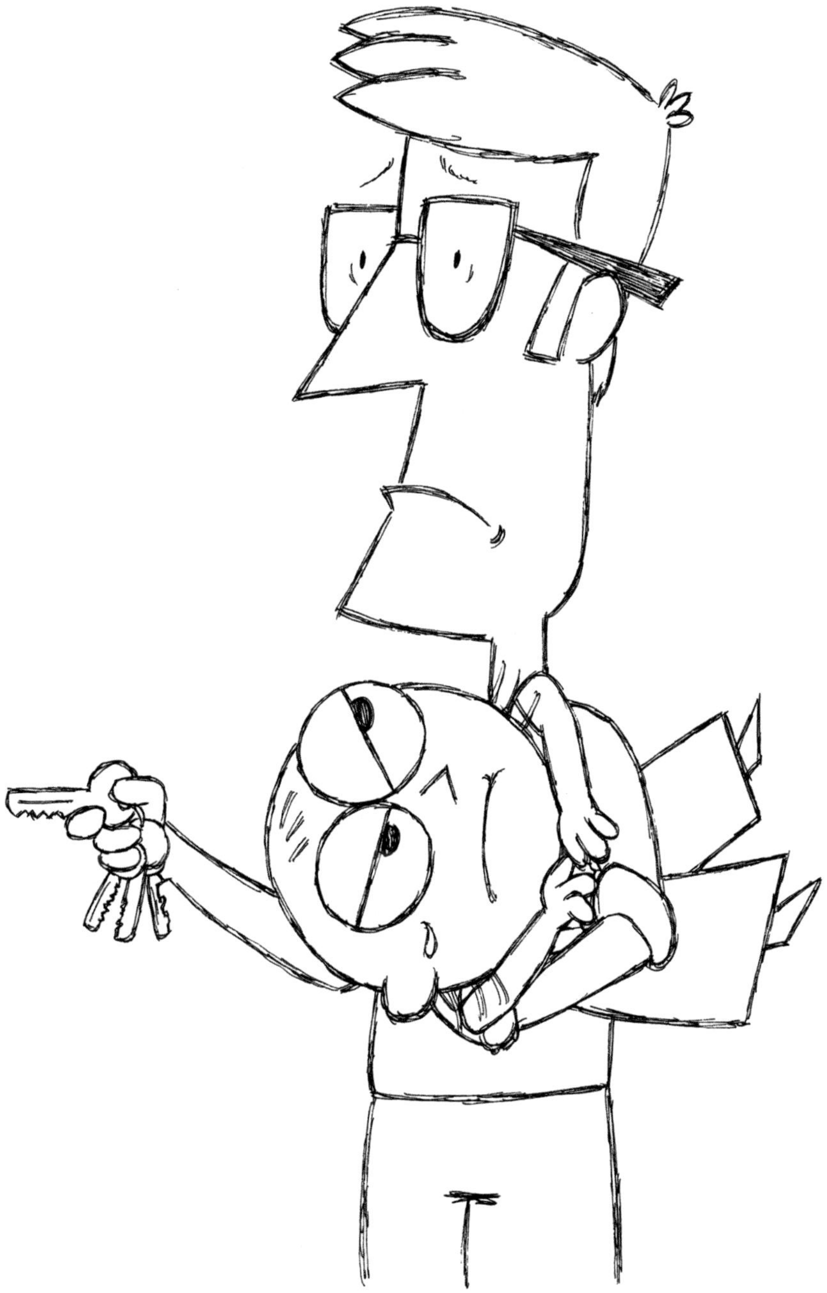

SERIOUSLY SILLY
A Decade of Art and Whimsy
by Mo Willems

The Eric Carle Museum of Picture Book Art
Amherst, Massachusetts June 22, 2013 – February 23, 2014

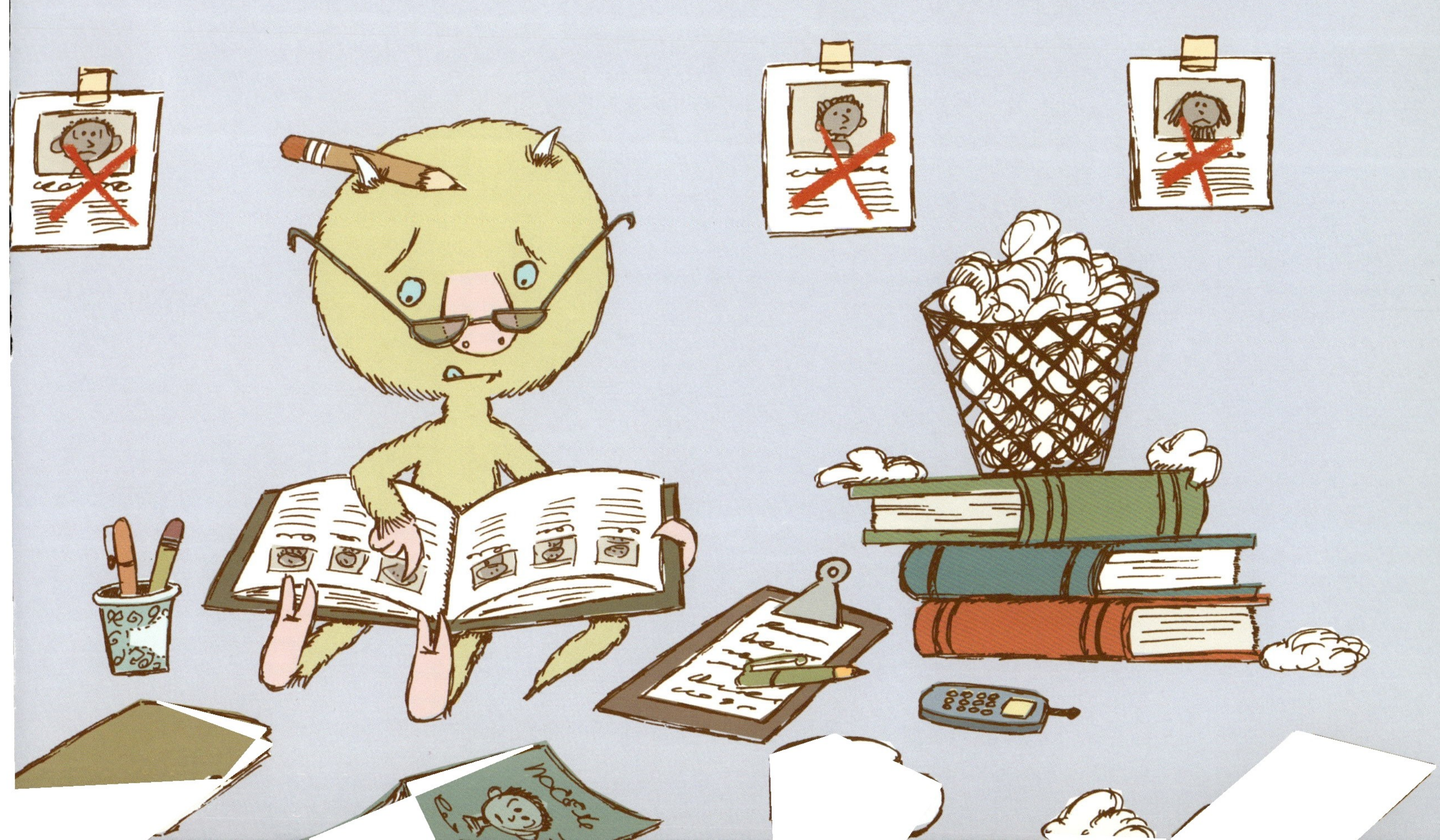

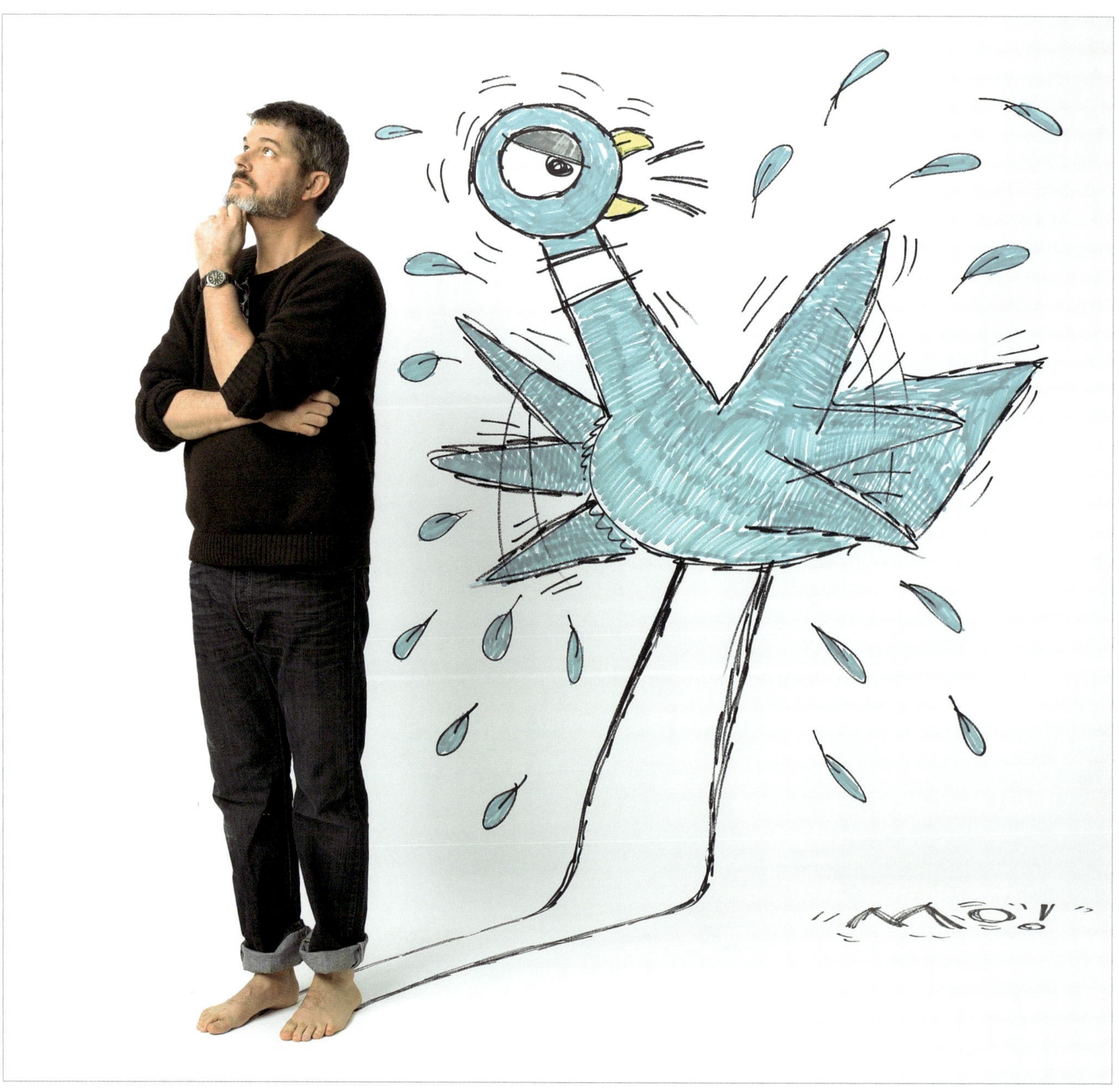

Photograph of Mo Willems by Marty Umans

The story is now well known. Ten years ago, a young writer from *Sesame Street* named Mo Willems published his first children's book— a sleeper about a pigeon hell-bent on getting behind the wheel of a bus. As adults, we secretly delight in the many ways that the pigeon's outbursts and wheedling echo those of the story's intended audience. But for our children the book was a revelation: Willems knew how to step aside so kids could make his books their own.

Let the pigeon drive the bus? *"Noooooo!"*

In one short decade, Willems has created more than 40 additional books for children and won three Caldecott Honors, two Theodor Seuss Geisel medals, and three Geisel Honors. Though it's still early in his career, he already has a place in children's book history, greatly influencing artists, writers, and publishers and reducing an entire generation to fits of giggling.

This summer, The Eric Carle Museum of Picture Book Art proudly presents a retrospective of his picture book work, *Seriously Silly: A Decade of Art and Whimsy by Mo Willems*. Chief Curator H. Nichols B. Clark, who organized the exhibition, has chosen almost a hundred works of art from the last ten years, some of them preliminary drawings that give viewers a glimpse of Willems's process and others finished illustrations that fully reveal his comedic genius. Willems's own work is accompanied by a selection of work by the comic book artists and cartoonists who have inspired him most, such as Charles M. Schulz, William Steig, and Saul Steinberg. Like the masters who came before him, Willems makes the simple look easy. "Put as little in as possible," he says.

This exhibition was made possible because of the generous support of Disney Publishing Worldwide. Nick Clark and I would like to especially thank Jeanne Mosure, Suzanne Murphy, Jennifer Corcoran, and their staffs for their enthusiasm and help as this exhibition came together over the last few years. We are also indebted to Alessandra Balzer, the first editor to recognize the power in a pigeon, and the Balzer + Bray staff at HarperCollins; to Richard Michelson of R. Michelson Galleries in Northampton, Massachusetts; and to Marcia Wernick of Wernick & Pratt Agency. A private collector who wishes to remain anonymous also generously lent us work.

We are grateful to Mo and Cheryl Willems in a hundred ways: for their many kindnesses throughout the exhibition process, for the generous loan of art from their private collection, and for their enduring interest in our work. *The Red Elephant*, a steel sculpture by Willems on extended loan to The Carle, is a daily reminder to us of their good humor and warmth.

Nick Clark and I would also like to personally thank the talented staff at The Carle, including the Collections team that put this exhibition together— Erica Jacob, Registrar & Collections Manager; Mark Bodah, Preparator; and Kristin Angel, Exhibitions Coordinator. We're not as funny as Mo is, but that never stops us from trying.

And from all of us at The Carle, our thanks once again to our founders, Eric and Barbara Carle. As far as we're concerned, they can drive the bus any time.

Alexandra Kennedy
Executive Director
The Eric Carle Museum of Picture Book Art

Don't Let the Pigeon Drive the Bus!

words and pictures by mo willems

Published cover for *Don't Let the Pigeon Drive the Bus!* 2003, Digital print

THE COMIC, THE CHARACTER, AND THE CRAFTSMAN IN THE ART OF MO WILLEMS

by H. Nichols B. Clark

Somewhere in Oxfordshire, England, there may still lurk a pigeon that has no idea what he or she hath wrought. Mo Willems had made a pilgrimage to Oxford in 1999 to write the great American picture book. He hoped the brainy environment would be a help, only to find himself mostly distracted by an irrepressible pigeon, who kept showing up in his sketch books. This encounter led, of course, to his first book, *Don't Let the Pigeon Drive the Bus!*, in 2003, which garnered a Caldecott Honor and launched Willems as one of the most popular and successful creators of children's books in the new century. This year marks the tenth anniversary of Willems's foray into this realm and provides a good moment to reflect on his prodigious accomplishments of the past decade.

While there are a few stand-alone books in the bibliography—notably *Time to Pee!*, *Leonardo the Terrible Monster*, and *Goldilocks and the Three Dinosaurs*—the core of his output comprises series, from the Pigeon and Knuffle Bunny to his early reader books featuring Elephant and Piggie and Cat the Cat. The hilariously comedic informs virtually all assessments of Willems's books and invariably refers back to his early calling in stand-up comedy and as a writer and animator for *Sesame Street*. Reviewers, revealing a commonality of observation, cite clean spare design, a minimalism, uncluttered illustrations and spare speech balloons, clarity, expressiveness, a sense of pacing, simplicity without being simplistic. They acknowledge a cartoonlike quality that certainly comes out of his earlier career in animation. To better understand this most recent chapter in Willems's career as an author and

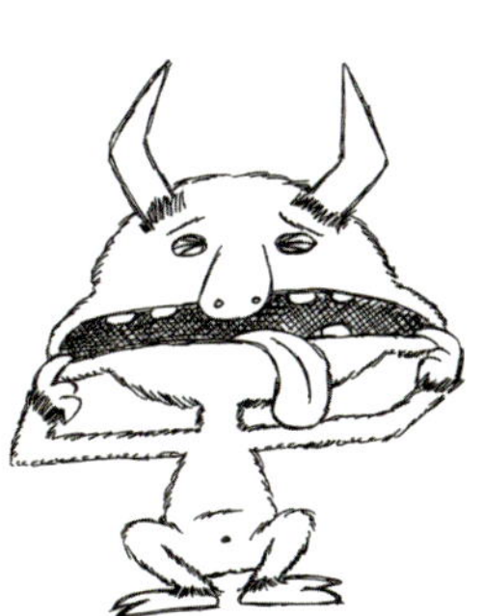
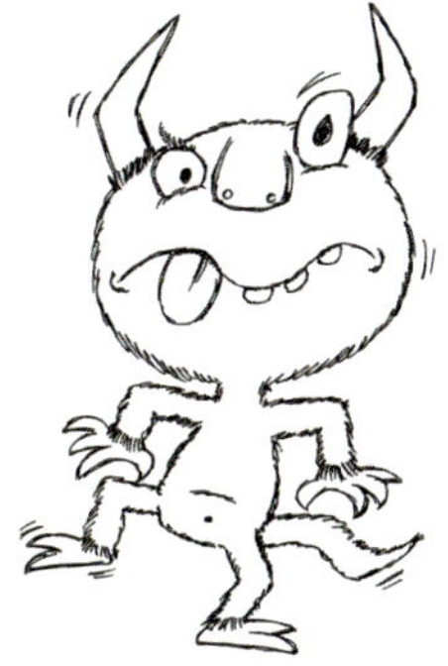
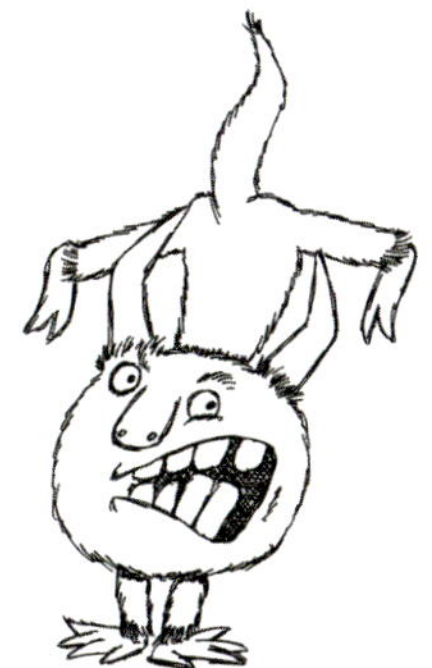

Leonardo The Terrible Monster, 7/7/04, Ink

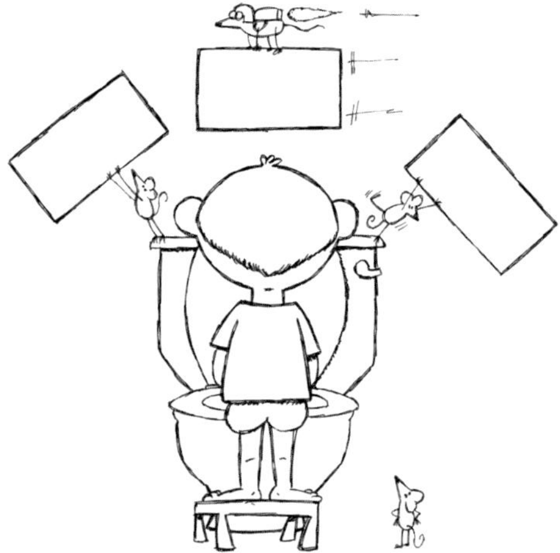

illustrator for young children, we need to quickly review aspects of his life.

By his own admission, Willems's childhood was not easy. As the only child of Dutch parents who immigrated to Chicago then settled in New Orleans, he was an outsider. He took great solace in the comics—especially *Peanuts* (he clearly identified with Charlie Brown)—and drawing. Charles Schulz was a hero, and Willems's formative style was guided by the reductive nature of the comic strip. Schulz's unvarnished perspective on human nature also impressed Willems, who early recognized the value of honesty—even if brutal—in telling a story. He also helped his father, a ceramic artist, in his studio and fully appreciated the significance of art as a functional craft. Indeed, to this day, Willems prefers to think of himself as a craftsman rather than an artist.

Since his family valued art, Willems was able to attend New York University's Tisch School to pursue a degree in filmmaking. In building his visual library, he watched a broad spectrum of films, including animated shorts ranging from the Bauhaus modernist aesthetic of Oskar Fichinger to the superb marriage of imagery and typography created by John and Faith Hubley. A short that especially resonated was *Gerald McBoing Boing*, adapted from a story by Dr. Seuss and produced by John Hubley. Curiously, in all of the interviews Willems has granted, no one has asked him about the importance of Dr. Seuss (who incidentally studied at Oxford). To my question, he responded, "Seuss was one of the few American authors I had in my house, so certainly his use of color and design made a big impression on me as a kid." Willems's early forays in film and animation embraced Seussian rhyming, and he admires Seuss's focus on "kids and humor;" he does fault him, however, for "sometimes ignoring emotional depth in his characters."

Ultimately, Willems resists influence from other picture-book artists, although he does express great admiration for

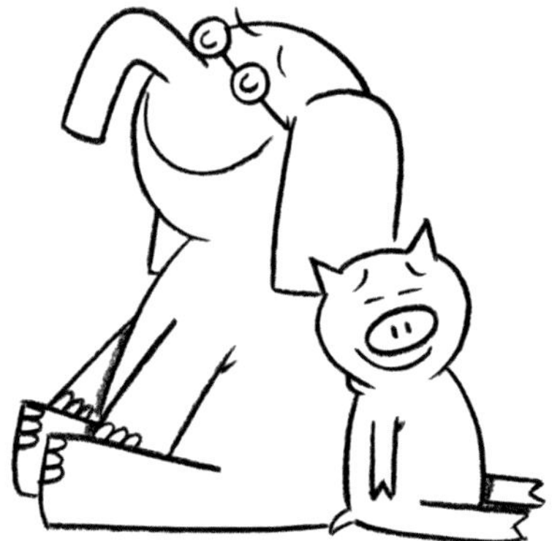

Time to Pee! 8/26/02, Ink
My Friend is Sad JAN 17 2006, Charcoal pencil

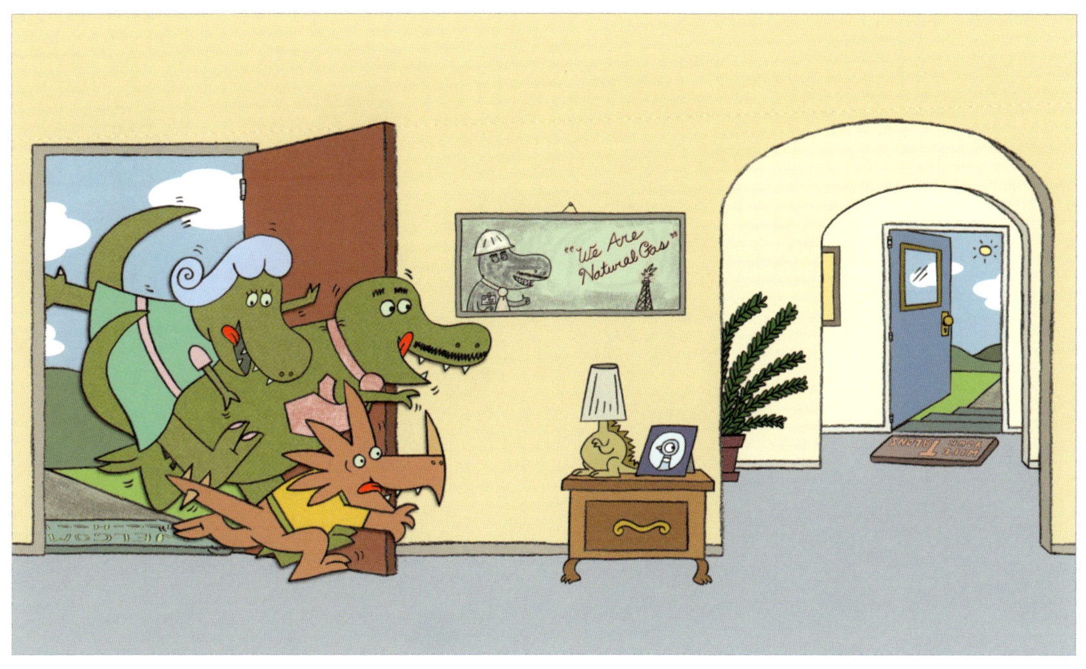

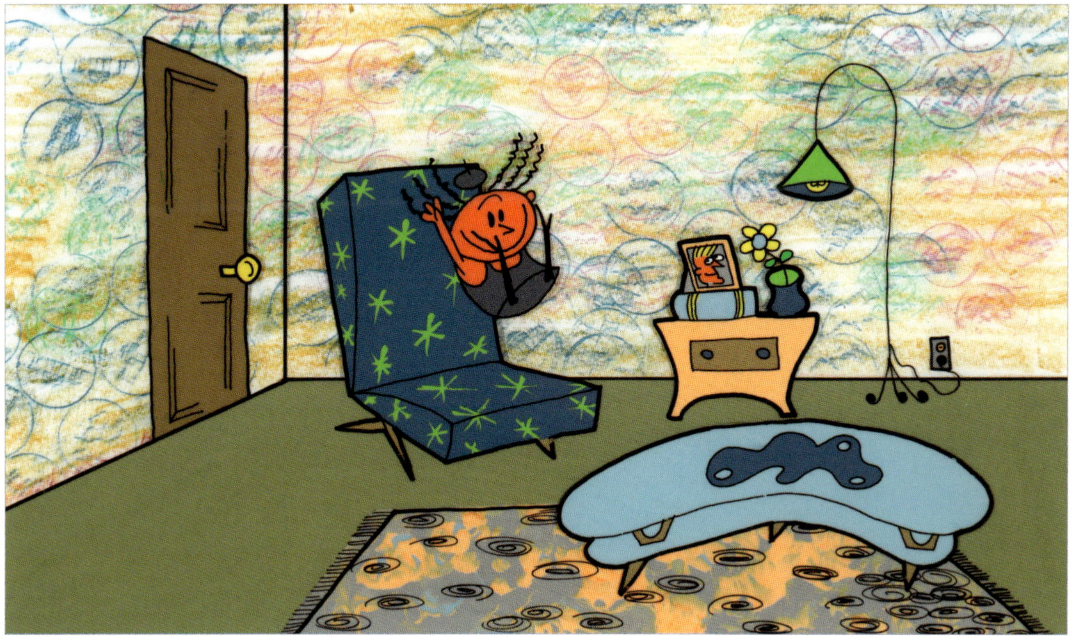

Published illustration for *Goldilocks and the Three Dinosaurs*, 2012, Digital print

Susie Kabloozie, 1994, Ink and cel paint on acetate

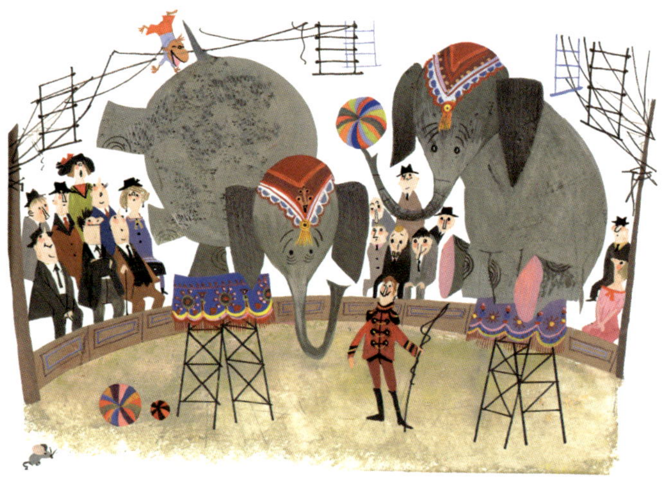

the legendary Dutch illustrator Fiep Westendorp and gravitates to people working in another genre, such as Bill Cosby and John Cleese. Central to these comedians and perhaps to all good comedy is humor at the expense of others. Willems quickly clarifies that such humor has to contain some of yourself, noting, "Writing, especially funny stuff, involves touching your own heart. But, to get there you have to rip open the rib cage and squeeze past the lungs. It can't help but be messy, shocking, and painful." In Willems's books there is often a crescendo of emotion, highlighted by large, often jagged type and expressive line that speaks directly to some of this passionate feeling—at which we cannot help but laugh.

The nine seasons he spent at *Sesame Street* honed a variety of skills, from writing humor to making animation under deadlines. In addition to producing vignettes of letters and numbers, Willems wrote a lot for Elmo and created Suzie Kabloozie. Consequently, he acquired the important skills of narrative, sequence, pacing, and timing. Animation attracted him because he wasn't at the mercy of live actors and uncooperative sets or weather. He was in control, and this was supremely important to him. He also created a couple of critically acclaimed independent shows, *The Off Beats* and *Sheep in the Big City*, that didn't catch on. In the words of a ten-year-old critic, "He tried too hard." Thus, when he decided to try a new career tack in the realm of children's books, he brought a very informed and formed vision to this calling.

Just as Willems is well grounded in the history of film, he is deeply passionate about art. He has acknowledged the importance of Picasso, Paul Klee, and Alexander Calder—coincidentally all artists who aspired to draw like children in search of an honesty and innocence. In addition to Charles Schulz, Willems also admires other cartoonists including Ronald Searle, Saul Steinberg, William Steig, and Jean-Jacques Sempé. They all share mordant wit conveyed with an economy of means. Realism does not resonate with him—not that he doesn't appreciate the likes of

Fiep Westendorp, *"Elephants in the Circus,"* ca. 1965, Digital print

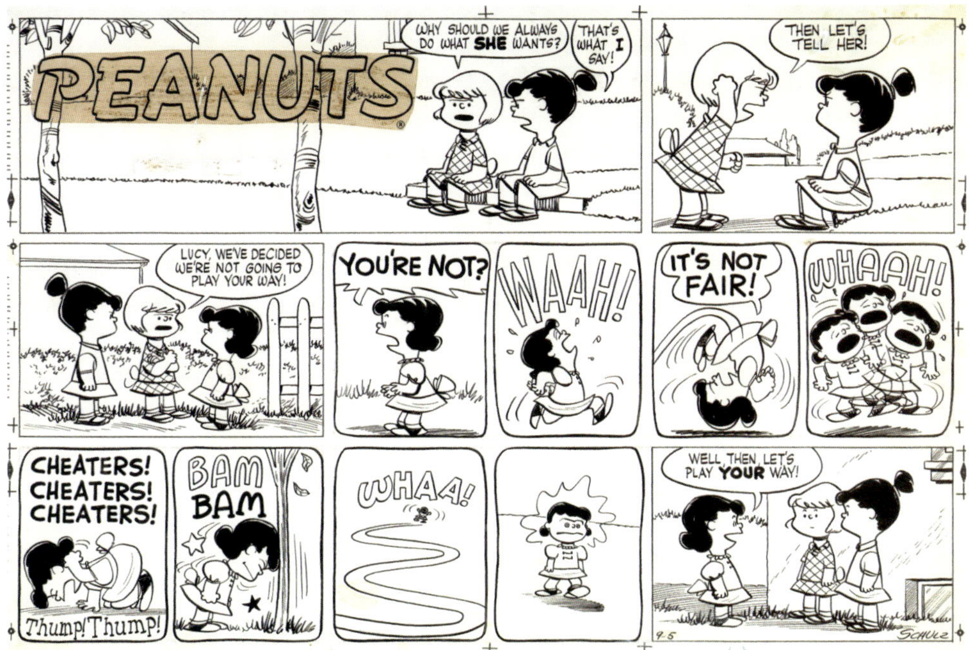

Rembrandt—but an accounting of the rooms he gravitates to in a museum is revealing: Islamic illustration, Turkish and Japanese calligraphy, Hindu sculpture, African masks, modern and contemporary art, musical instruments, as well as the design work of Isamu Noguchi and Charles Eames.

This seriousness of purpose is also reflected in his library, which ranges from a substantial collection of books on the masters of cartooning—American, British, and Continental—to a selective gathering of volumes about art and artists he especially admires, including Hieronymous Bosch, Paul Klee, Ben Shahn, Joan Mirò, and an intriguing publication titled *Naïve: Modernism and Folklore in Contemporary Graphic Design*. Another telling volume from his extensive collection of books on history is Neil MacGregor's *A History of the World in 100 Objects*. Clearly Willems is attracted to telling big stories very selectively.

There are connective tissues here: variety of line weight in the calligraphy, planarity in the sculpture, two-dimensionality and abstraction in the modern art, and a marriage of the practical and purity of form in the design components and musical instruments. It is all a distilling down to the bare minimum—less is more—and this is a key tenet of Willems's art whatever the story. He says, "I'm more interested in graphic simplifications that serve as metaphor. I'd rather my work look immediate than time consuming." And this, of course, is so terribly misleading. One can look at Willem's finished work and say, "but it is so simple." And yes, he empowers everyone to draw the pigeon, but when

Charles Schulz, *"April 1 Peanuts with Good 'ol' Charlie Brown,"* April 1, 1953, Pen and ink

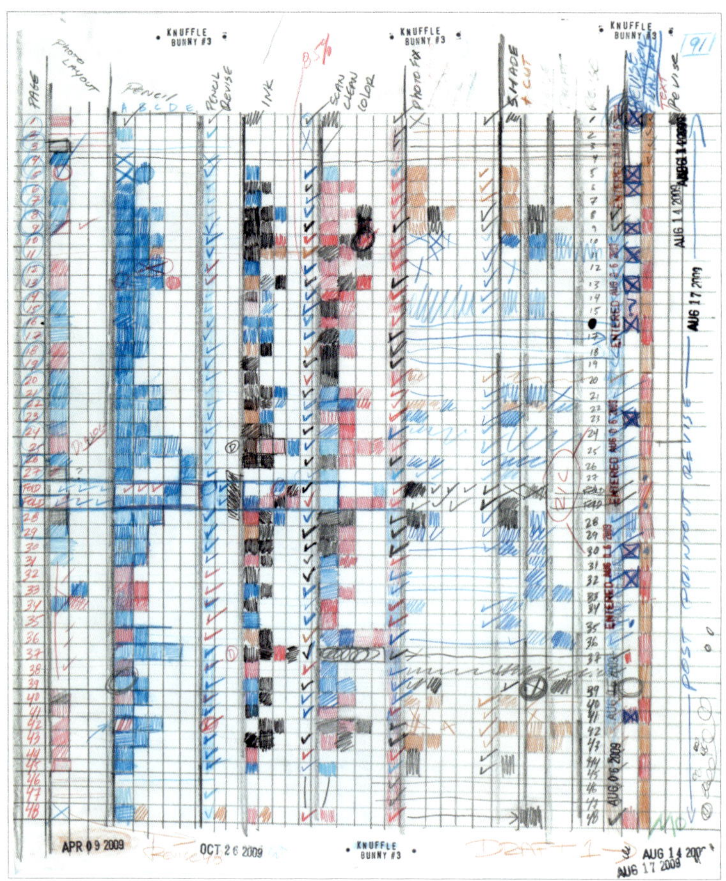

you dig through his flat files and realize the unrelenting process he subscribes to (a perusal of one of his work sheets testifies to his almost obsessive nature), you quickly realize the path he takes is anything but easy. He is on a quest for an exquisite balance where a single word or a single line can over-explain or oversimplify the narrative or visual text. He wants his books to have just enough of a visual springboard to launch readers on their own creative endeavors. The seemingly easy is informed by repetition and disappointment. As Willems suggests, "You never know when it's right, but with enough practice you can smell when it's wrong. The key is to keep working until it no longer smells wrong. That's something that comes with practice and multiple failures."

As noted, a pigeon was the catalyst that helped Willems create children's books and extend his background in animation—especially the emphasis of the two-dimensional. The pigeon ranks among the smartest and most persevering of birds; one even was awarded the Croix de Guerre (one of

Workflow chart for *KNUFFLE BUNNY, TOO, A Case of Mistaken Identity,* ca. 2006, Mixed media

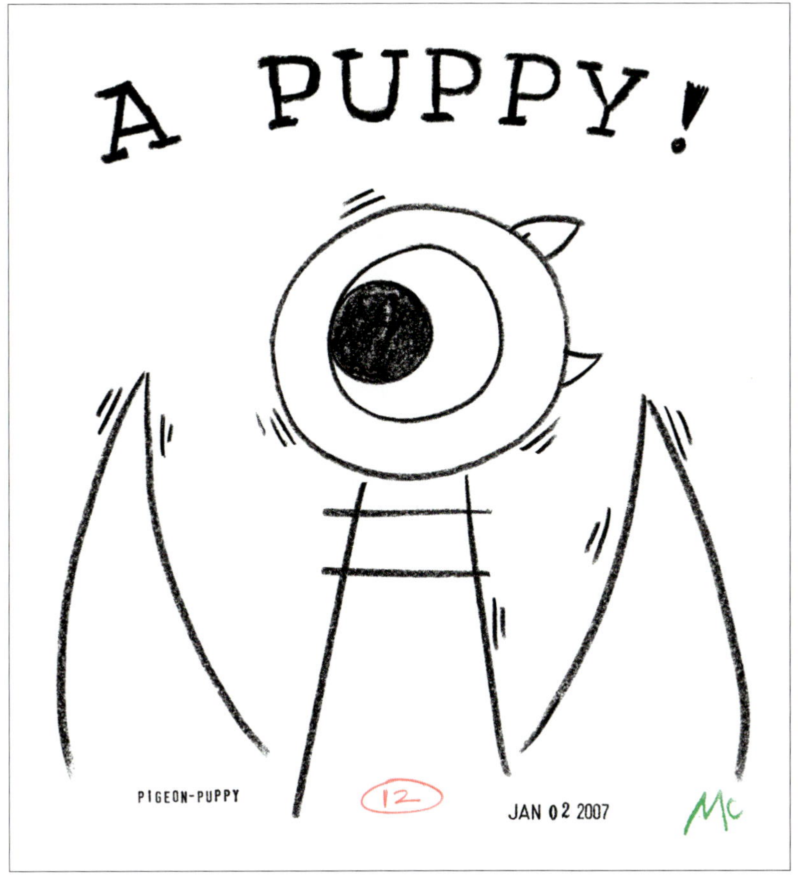

the highest French military honors) for valor in World War I. Thus, that chance encounter with the pigeon in Oxford may have been more than Willems bargained for. Indeed, the pigeon still calls the shots and tells the artist when it is time for another book about him. Clearly, Willems didn't burden his pigeon with extraneous visual baggage. The neck and head, when viewed in profile, recall the reductive visual process of Picasso during his period of Analytic Cubism from 1909 to 1912 when he was bent on paring objects down to their most essential geometries. While this was a hermetic, intellectual exercise, Picasso also said his most cherished goal was to draw like a child to achieve their innocence and directness.

For creating this maiden effort, Willems reflected on his turning to the gold standard—Maurice Sendak—for guidance. In a memorial tribute, he acknowledged the importance of Sendak's masterpiece, recalling, "*Where the Wild Things Are* is rightly considered the pinnacle of children's picture books, for its structure, draftsmanship, and content. Certainly, I used the book as a template for my first effort,

The Pigeon Wants a Puppy!, JAN 02 2007, Aquarelle pencil

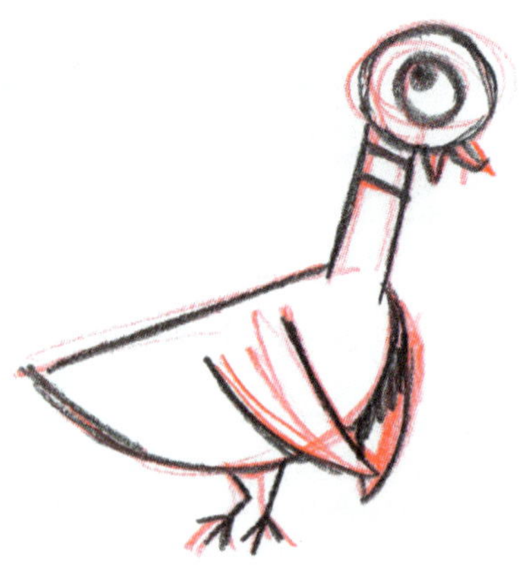

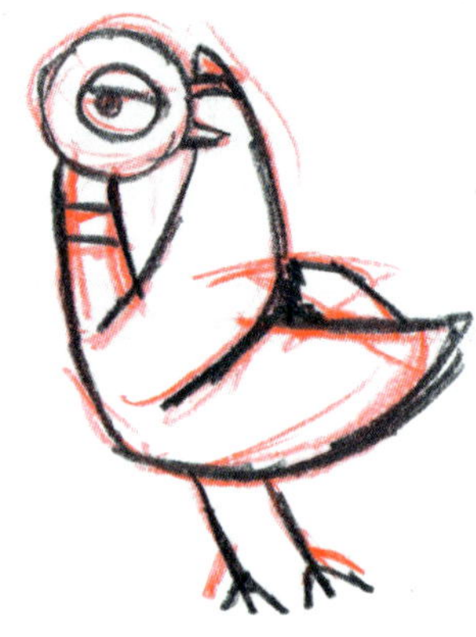

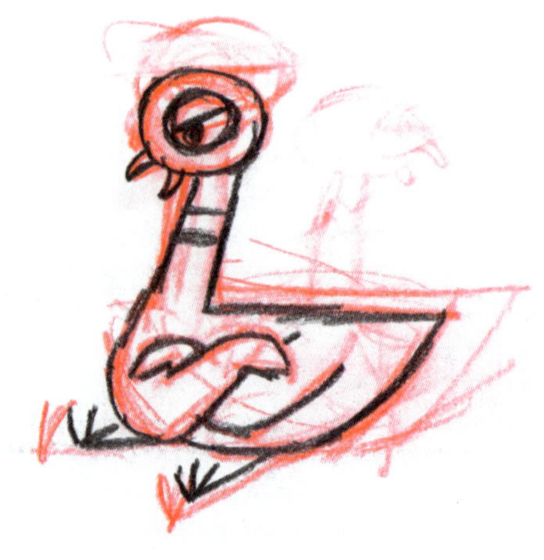

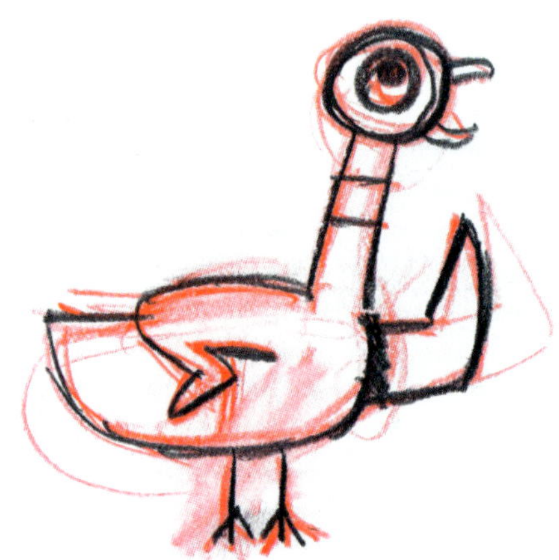

Don't Let the Pigeon Drive the Bus!, 1/31/02, Graphite, red pencil, printed and pasted text

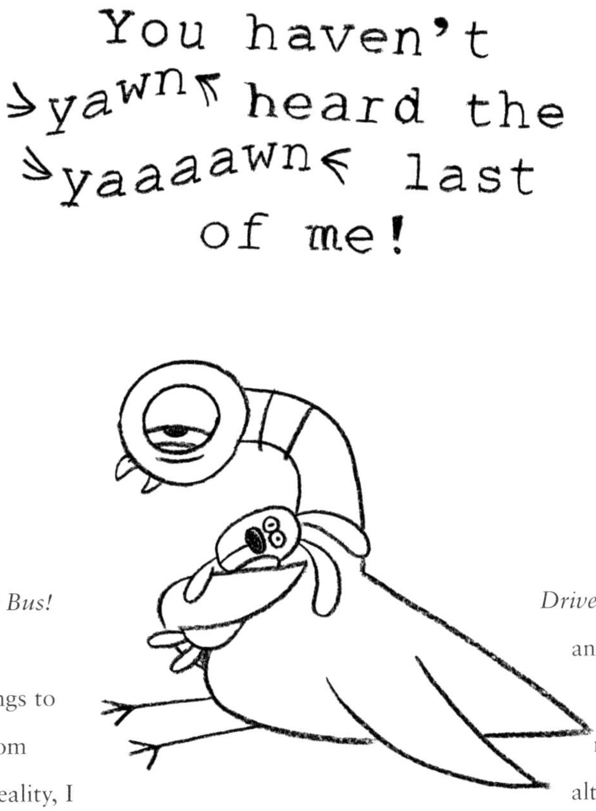

You haven't yawn heard the yaaaawn last of me!

Don't Let the Pigeon Drive the Bus! Where Sendak increased and decreased the size of the drawings to indicate the slide of emotion from reality to fantasy and back to reality, I used colored backgrounds to underline the character's emotional state. If you're going to steal an idea, steal from the best, right?"

Whatever the pigeon's objective, and there are many—driving a bus, eating a hot dog, staying up late, getting a puppy—Willems provides the consummate touch by revealing mood and emotion through the most understated composition. He has no inclination to create a three-dimensional world on a two-dimensional surface. It is his training in animation that comes to the fore. In *Don't Let the Pigeon Drive the Bus!* Willems incorporates the animation process of generating the preliminary idea in blue pencil and making subsequent corrections and alterations in red. The working sketch for "I'll be your best friend!" and the three other vignettes on that sheet reveal Willems working out the poses, gestures, and expressions in red pencil before capturing the next iteration in black pencil. The final resolution is rendered in black grease pencil. One can easily note that Willems is still searching for just the right facial expression. Of critical importance—and this holds true for all of his characters—is the placement of the pupil within the eye. For Willems this detail is of paramount importance in assuring the expression captures the tenor of the moment. Willems,

Don't Let the Pigeon Stay Up Late!, 1/03/05, Aquarelle pencil

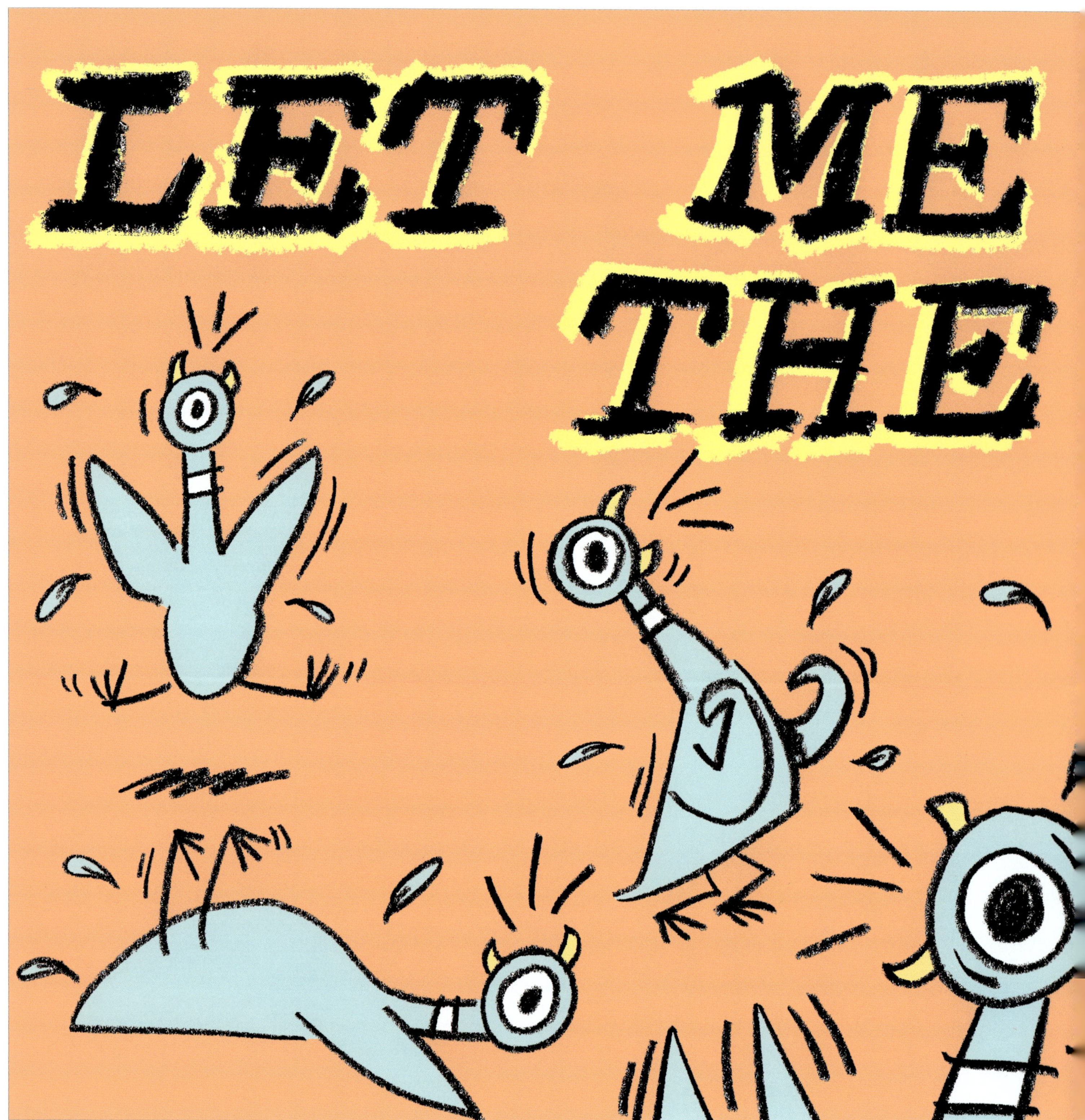
LET ME
THE

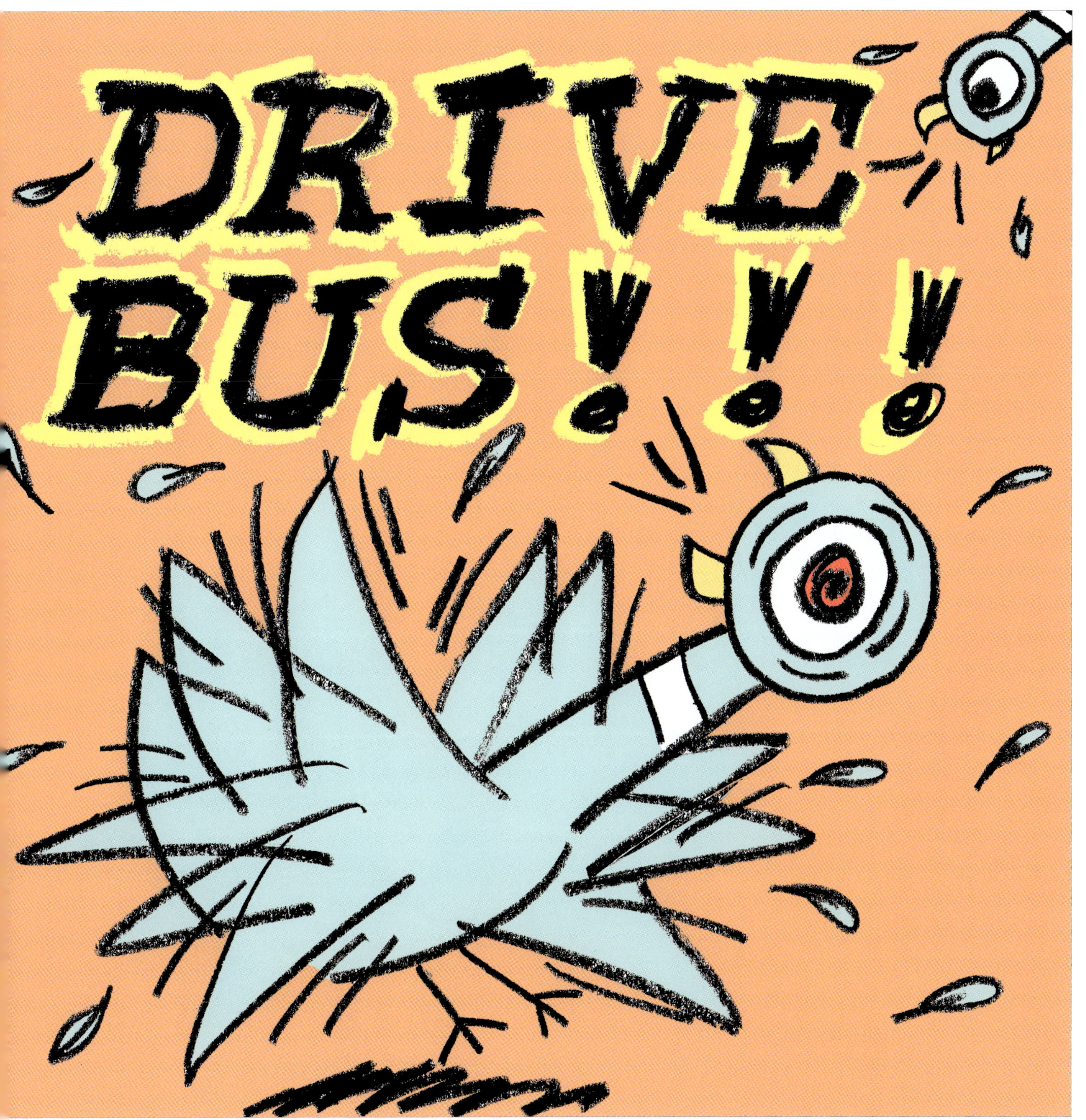

Published illustration for *Don't Let the Pigeon Drive the Bus!*, 2003, Digital print

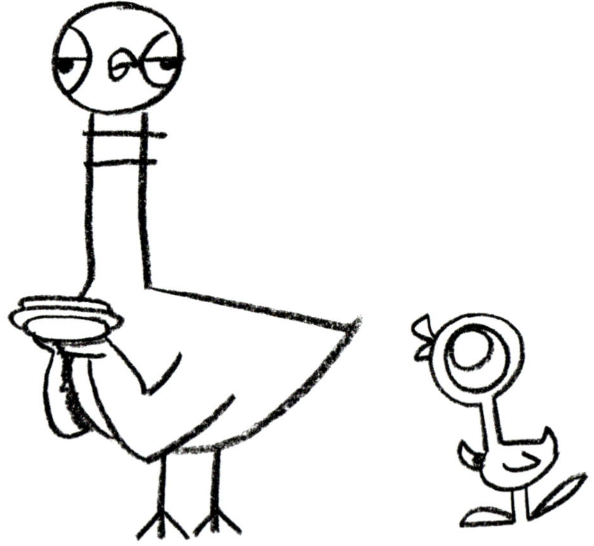

of course, is not alone in this concern and propensity. Maurice Sendak expressed appreciation for Randolph Caldecott, whose ability to capture remarkable expressiveness with the most minimal of means—often just dashes for the eyes, but what dashes!—sets the bar very high.

From the outset, Willems imbued the pigeon with great personality and not a little chutzpah. What especially engages the young reader is the apparent shifting of roles; they are the ones who can say, "**NO!**" And this is central to Willems's objectives; he receives a lot of mail from his young fans offering fertile suggestions about what **not** to let the pigeon do. Such engagement is at the core of his aspirations—to involve the reader—to inspire them to make their own stories and their own drawings. To let their imaginations take flight.

Willems introduces a diminutive duckling in the second book, *The Pigeon Finds a Hot Dog!*, and this charming character provides a delightful foil of understatement to the pigeon's bombast. Invariably where Pigeon fails to have his way, Duckling succeeds, and this culminates in the most recent book in the series, *The Duckling Gets a Cookie!?* Duckling employs the magic word in quest of a cookie and is rewarded for his politesse. Pigeon is incredulous that it was so easy for Duckling, and incredulity is compounded by astonishment when Duckling gives **him** the cookie. Thus many of life's important lessons—in this case civility and generosity—are delivered in the guise of slapstick theater.

The Knuffle Bunny trilogy deals with universals of parenting—who of us with children hasn't suffered through the temporary absence of a child's beloved blankie or bunny or

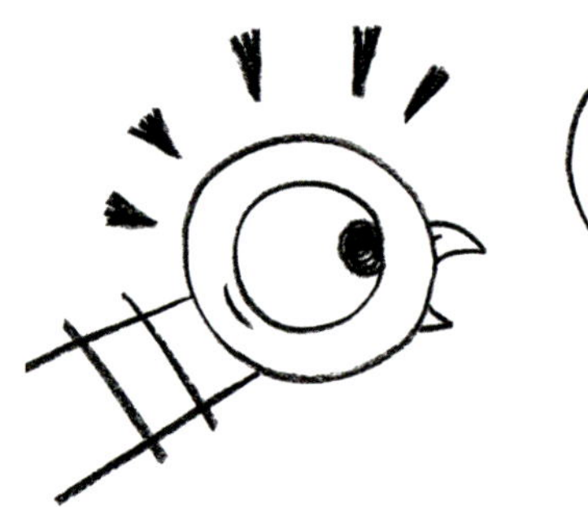

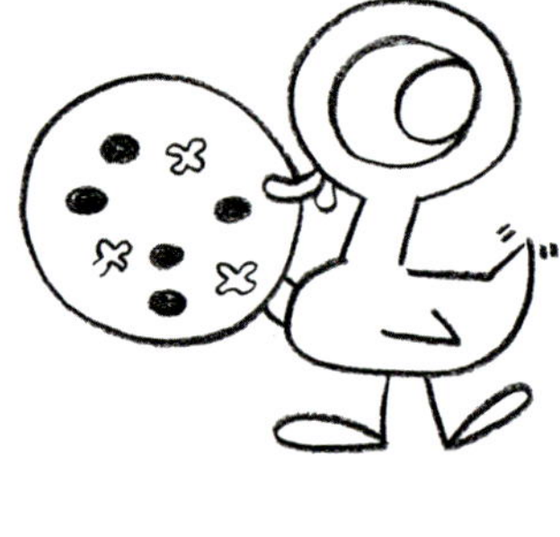

The Pigeon Finds a Hot Dog!, 3/19/03, Aquarelle pencil
Cover for *The Duckling Gets a Cookie!?*, DEC 08 2010, Aquarelle pencil

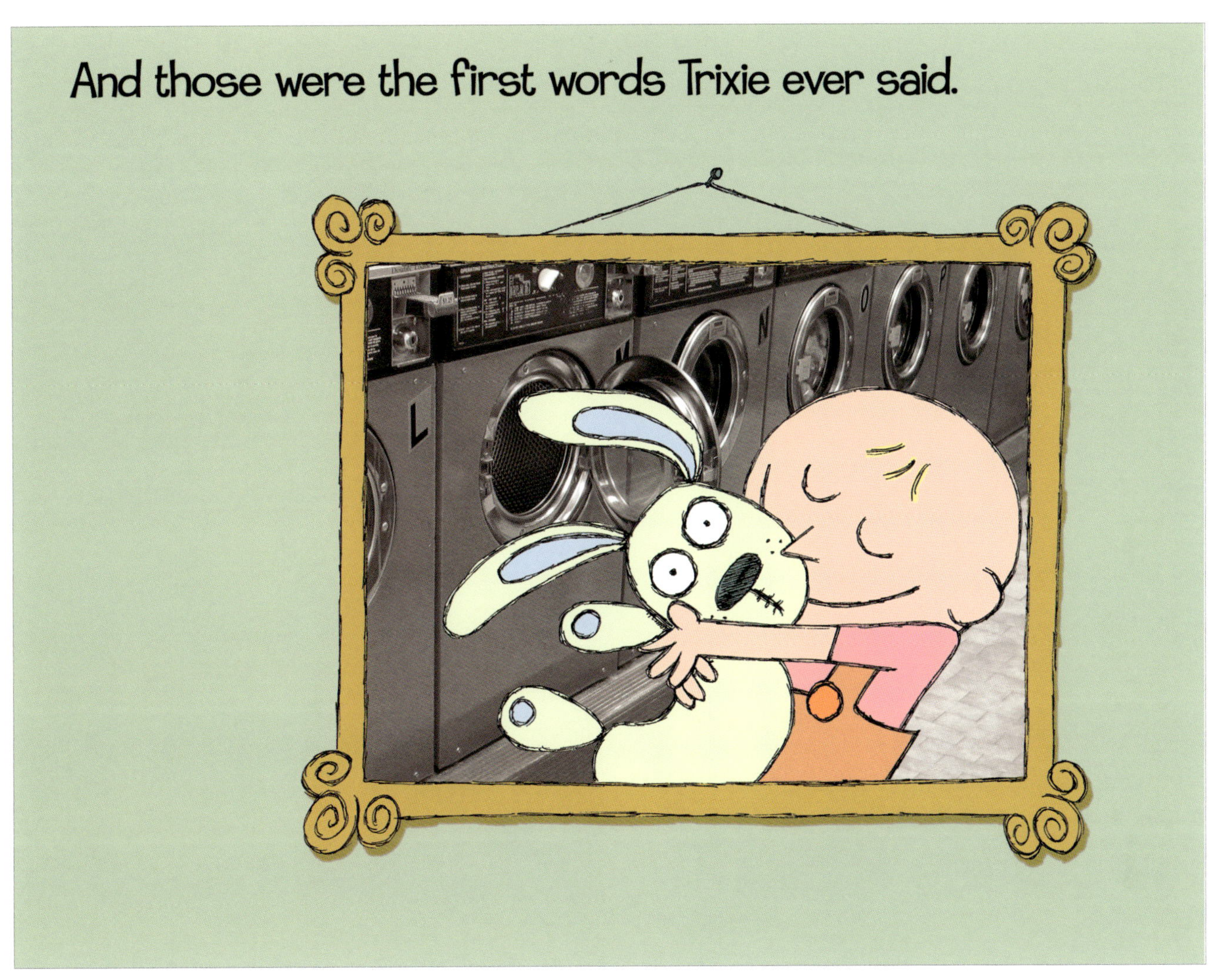

Published illustration for *KNUFFLE BUNNY, A Cautionary Tale*, 2004, Digital print

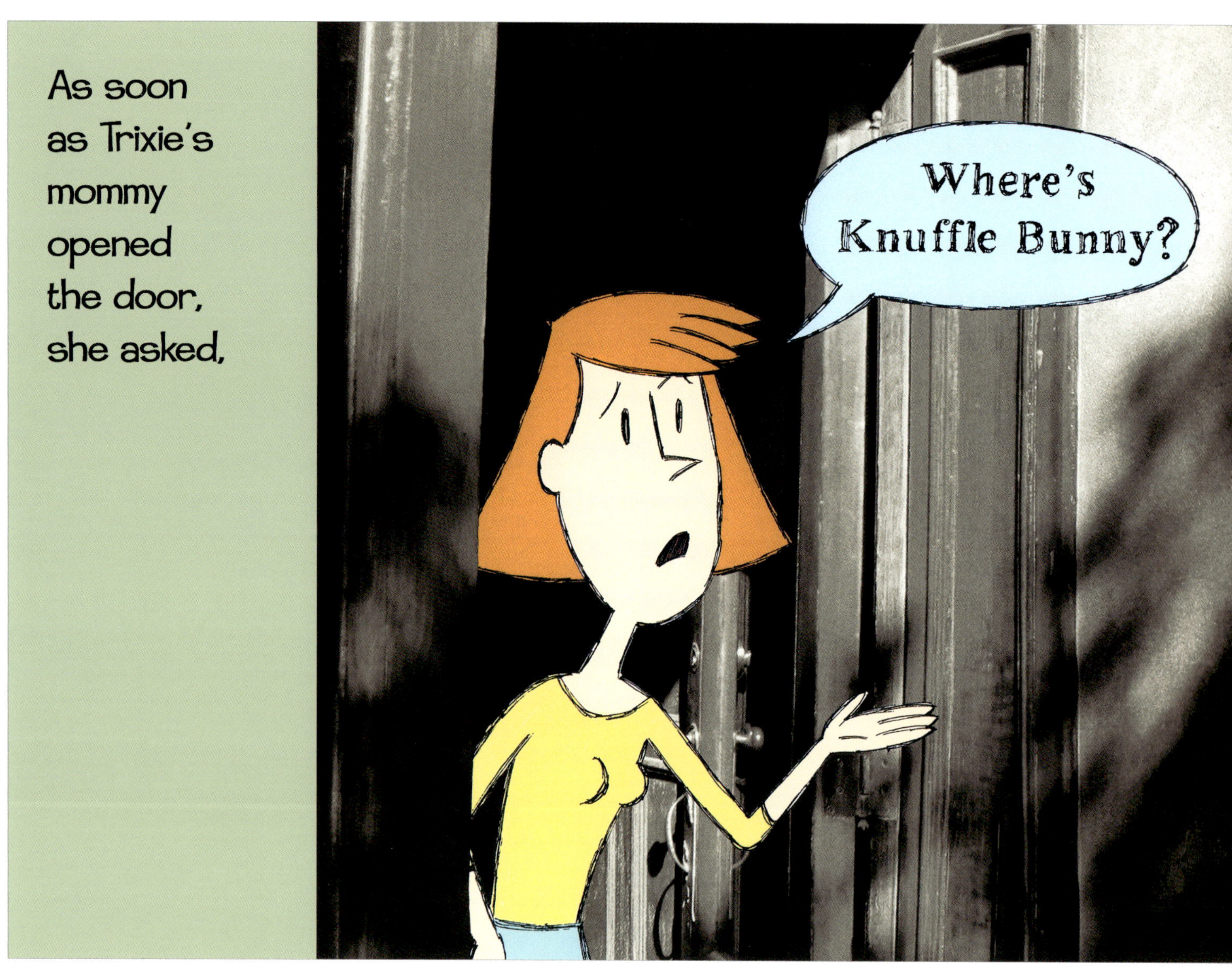

bear? And who hasn't celebrated that rite of passage when whatever shred remains is finally consigned to the wastebasket or scrapbook? And Willems skillfully provides the message from the child's point of view. In the first book in the series, Dad gets bonus points for doing the laundry at the Laundromat. He then squanders them by losing track of his pre-verbal daughter's beloved Knuffle Bunny. Mom, of course, comes to the rescue, and all's well that ends well.

Willems quickly hits his stride in terms of his artistic approach, and the fully formed animation process takes

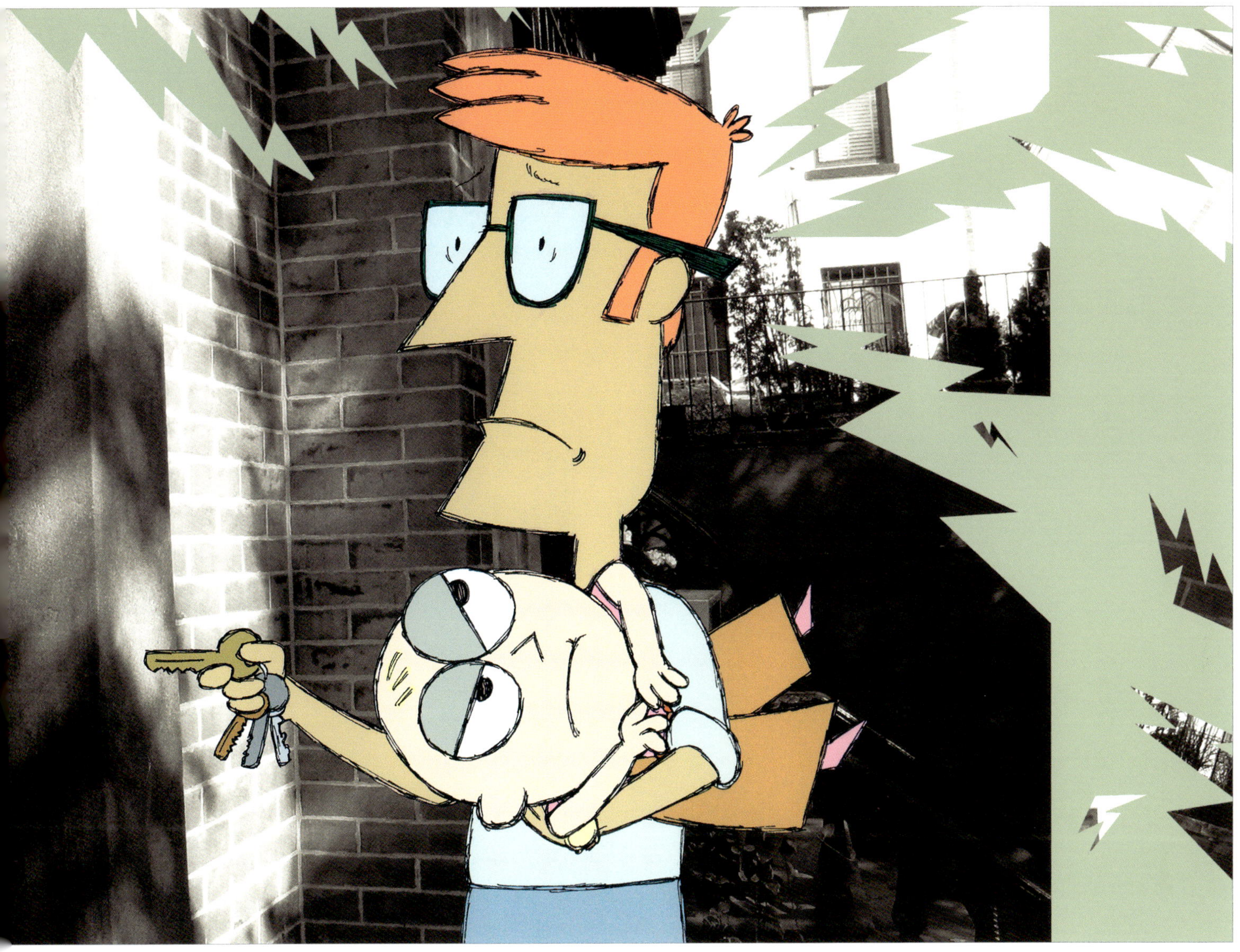

hold. We see the elegant and very legible process of blue to red pencil to finished ink captured so effectively. The artist also gravitates to the siren call of mixed media, using photographs of Brooklyn streets for the setting. That this might save him time and effort proved illusory, and he spent a lot of time cleaning up the photos to achieve just the right ambience. He contends, "The emotional truth is more important than the physical truth. When details divert the eye and emotion from the emotional content, they need to go." Here again, it is all about the process of distillation.

Published illustration for *KNUFFLE BUNNY, A Cautionary Tale*, 2004, Digital Print

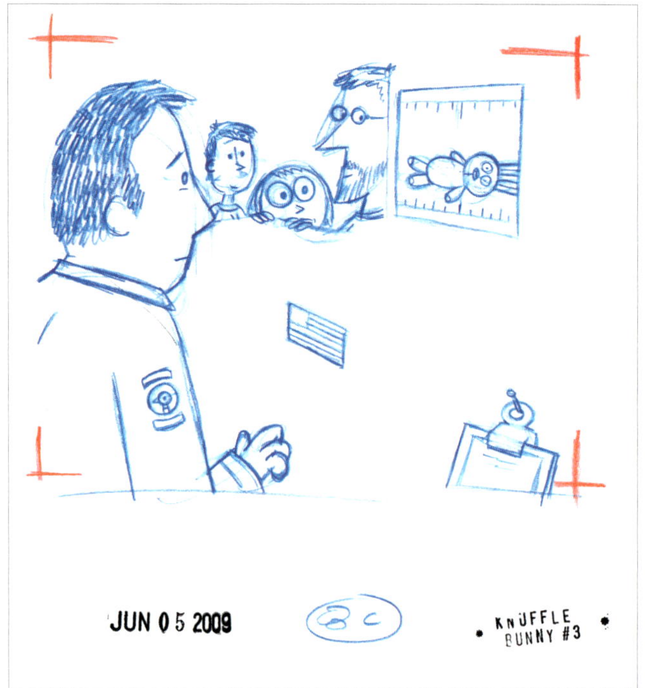

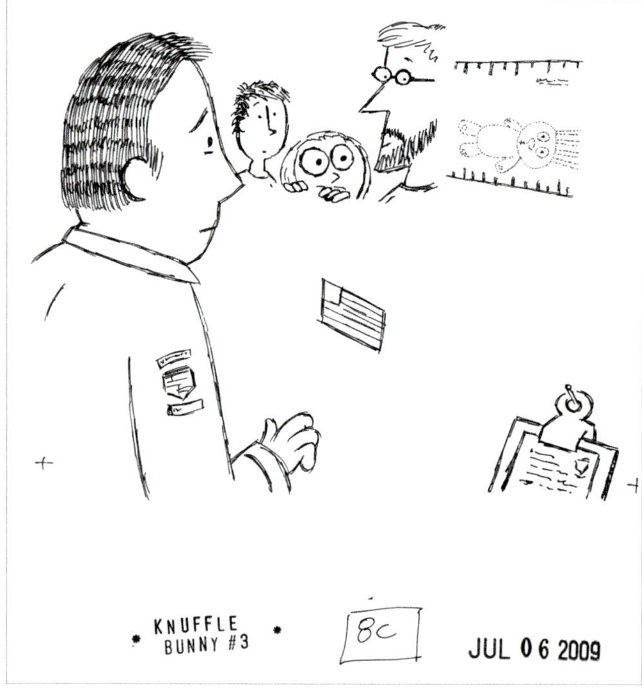

The middle book, *Knuffle Bunny Too*, addresses the vexing situation of two children having the identical bunny. The story tells of jealousy, mistaken identity, middle-of-the-night calls, restitution, and most importantly the forging of new friendships. Again, Willems demonstrates his mastery of presenting profound issues with a velvet glove.

The final book, *Knuffle Bunny Free*, considers that transformative moment when the beloved stuffed animal (or blankie) is no longer the central defining aspect of a child's life. An international flight to visit family in the Netherlands triggers this realization. Willems had to go to extraordinary ends to ensure that his photographic settings were accurate. In one instance, this goal presented a seemingly insurmountable hurdle: Willems wanted to show Knuffle Bunny going through the x-ray machine at airport security. Understandably, the Transportation Security Administration was a bit touchy about the artist photographing their security measures, so Willems turned to his friend Jon Scieszka, who was serving as National Ambassador for Young People's Literature, to see if he could cut some red tape. Scieszka happily obliged. What is so visually arresting is how Trixie's eyes and those of Knuffle Bunny echo the same

Left: *KNUFFLE BUNNY FREE, An Unexpected Diversion*, JUN 05 2009, Blue and red colored pencil
Right: *KNUFFLE BUNNY FREE, An Unexpected Diversion*, JUL 06 2009, Ink

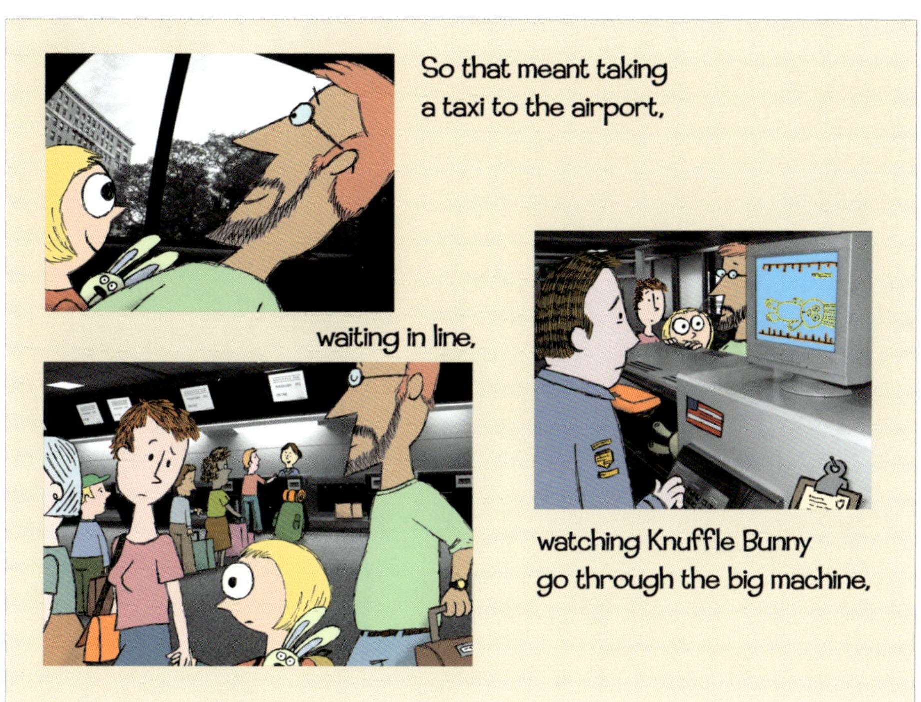

wide-eyed sense of anxiety.

Another lovely touch—and yet another example of pigeon power—is Willems's ongoing inclusion of the pigeon in his books—reminiscent of the cameos Alfred Hitchcock made in his movies. Initially, Willems placed the pigeon on the official patch on the right shoulder of the TSA officer, but this didn't make it to the final rendering. Instead Pigeon shows up as the logo of Opa's reusable shopping bag and later in book form back in Trixie's room at home. Others of Willems's characters make occasional sly appearances, but Pigeon is pervasive. That Knuffle Bunny survived intact to be passed along is a tribute to Trixie's careful attention and its durability—or perhaps it's poetic license. The trilogy ends on a lovely note of the generational cycle of Knuffle Bunny's attachment to the very young.

While books in series comprise the bulk of Willems's output, he has on occasion created "stand-alone" books that carry their own important messages for children in very engaging terms. Willems addresses the rite of passage of toilet training and mastering control over bodily functions in *Time to Pee!* (where incidentally there is a toy bus being

Published illustration for *KNUFFLE BUNNY FREE, An Unexpected Diversion*, 2010, Digital print

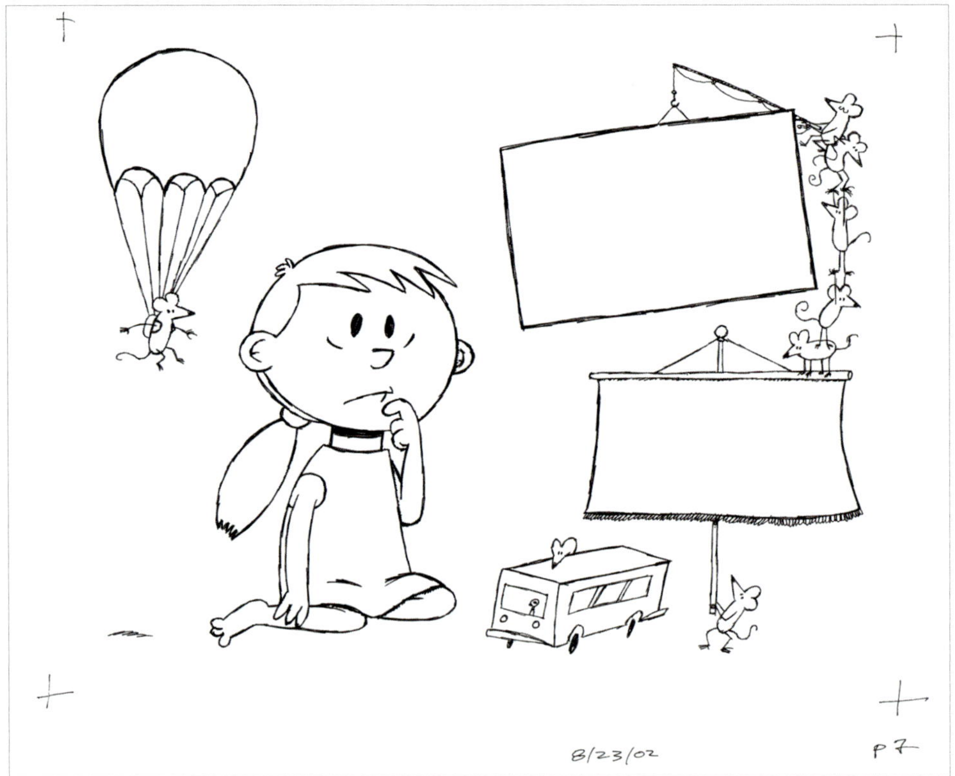

driven by you-know-who). The potentially awkward subject is provided great levity by the supporting cast of hilarious mice whose zany antics defuse the real business at hand. Willems has framed the text in a succession of colored placards that anticipate this use in his Elephant and Piggie easy readers. The device cleverly isolates the words yet sets them in a playful context.

Manners are an ongoing concern of the artist, and consciously or not he continues a long and distinguished tradition in this genre. Willems focuses on the difference that saying "Please" can make, and he continues the contrivance of placing text into a variety of relevant shapes, with the mice assisting in their display. Whether it is getting a turn on the bucking pigeon or scoring a chocolate chip cookie, "Please" opens lots of doors, while "Excuse me" and "Sorry!" serve as important codas to this essay in good manners. Sequence, legibility, and pacing are continued key ingredients to reinforcing these ineluctable mores.

Friends seem to have been hard to come by in Willems's childhood, so it is not surprising that friendship is a recurrent theme in his books, whether in series or the stand

Time To Pee!, 8/23/02, Ink

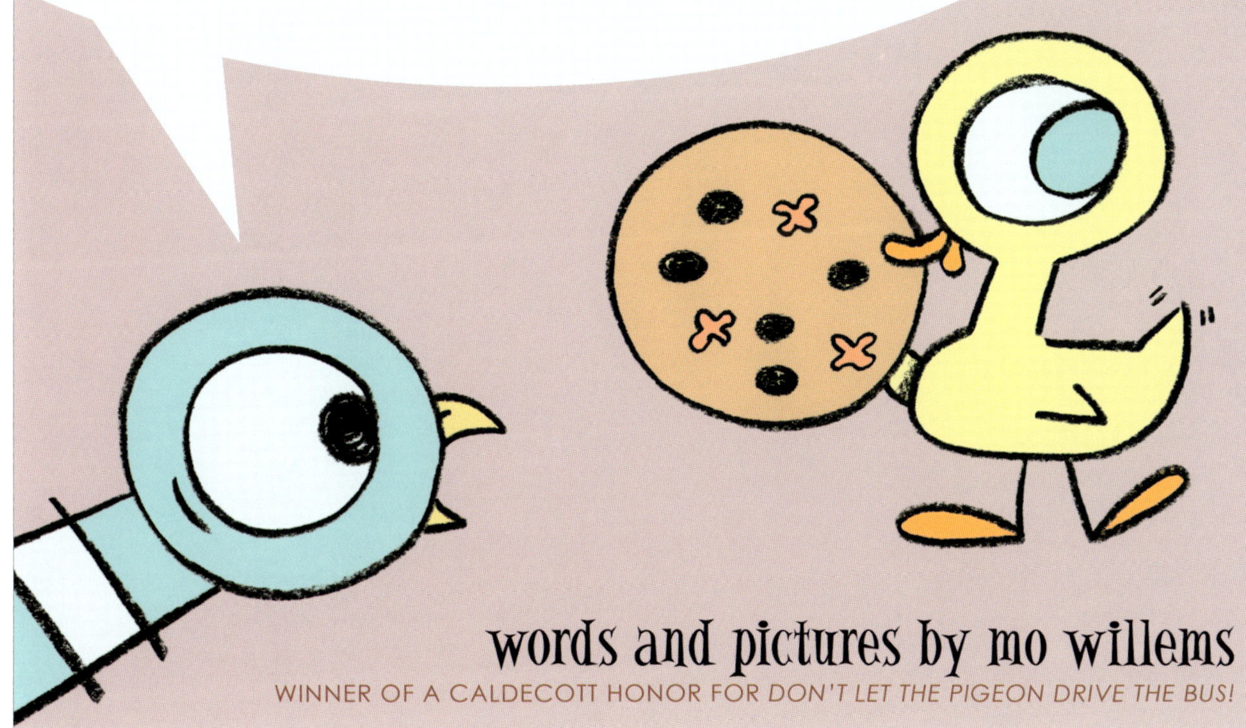

Published cover for *The Duckling Gets a Cookie!?*, 2012, Digital print

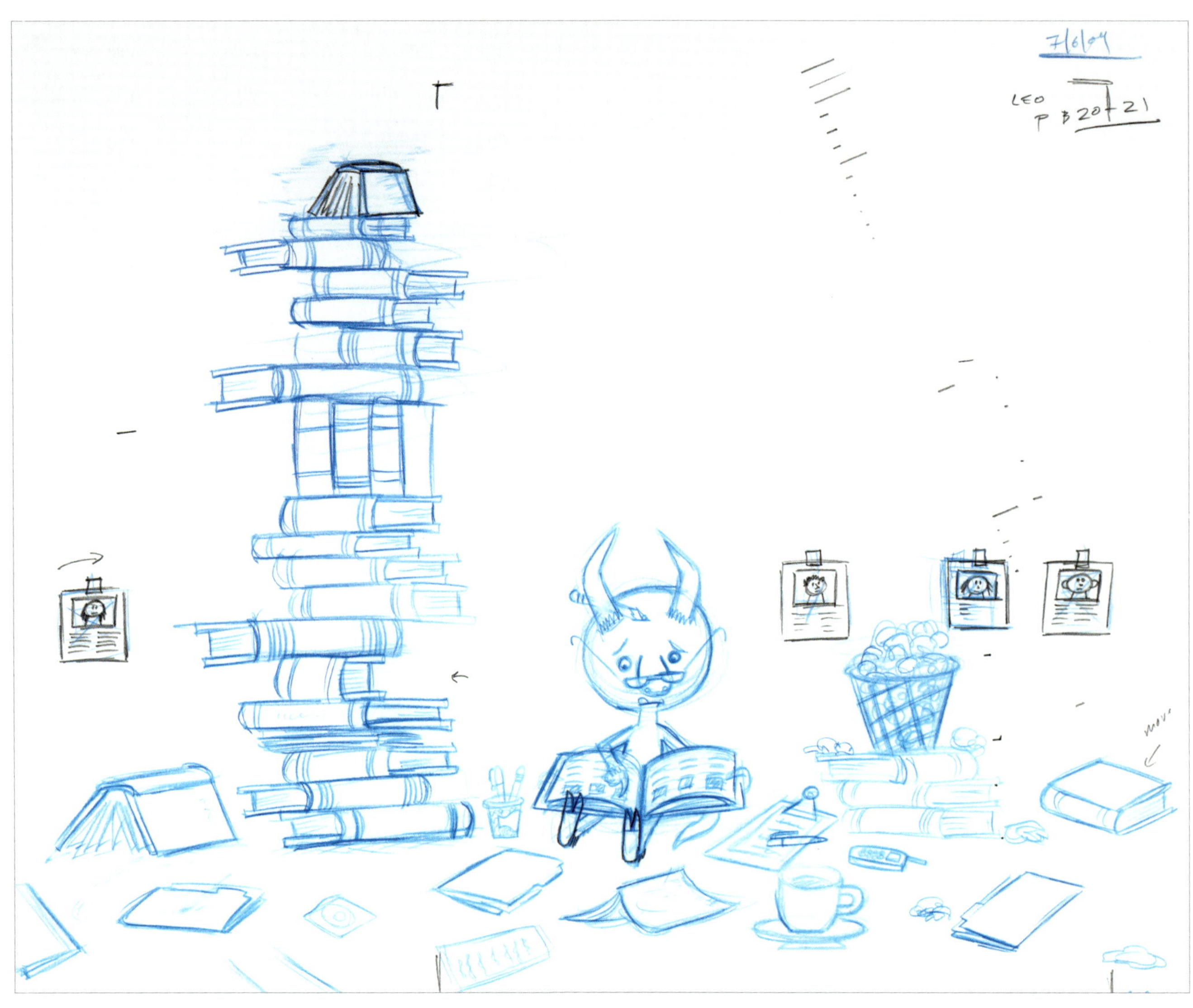

Leonardo the Terrible Monster, 7/6/04, Graphite and blue pencil

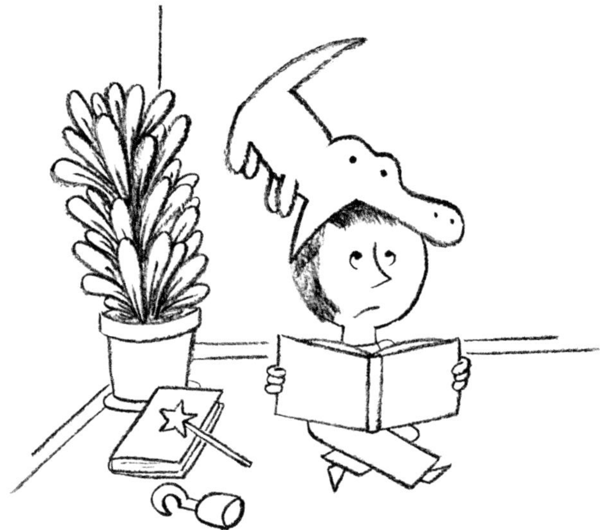

alones. He often comes at the notion from a wonderfully oblique angle. In *Leonardo the Terrible Monster*, the protagonist suffers an abject sense of failure since he cannot scare anyone—even someone he determines is the most timid person he can find. But this ultimate flop leads to a friendship that more than compensates for his futile past. In *Edwina The Dinosaur Who Didn't Know She Was Extinct* the rationale is tested by the presence of a beloved dinosaur who is part playmate to all the children and part girl scout—helping old ladies across the street and baking chocolate chip cookies (a clear culinary leitmotif in the Willems oeuvre). When Reginald Van Hoobie-Doobie lays out the empirical data about dinosaurs being extinct, he learns people don't really care even in the face of those facts, and his hostility morphs to friendship. *Hooray For Amanda & Her Alligator!* constitutes a partial tip of the hat to *Calvin and Hobbes* in the vivid relationship between a child and her stuffed animal. The overarching message, however, addresses sibling rivalry when Amanda brings a stuffed panda home from her visit to the zoo. Alligator doesn't take it well, but eventually comes around—as one hopes most young children do who are confronted with a younger sibling. The artist uses a minimum of means within a very playful context to convey this complex and often confusing idea. Willems has a wonderfully facile way of communicating with his young audience.

From friendship Willems moves to unorthodoxy and ostracism in *Naked Mole Rat Gets Dressed*. Haberdashery was not one of the tenets in the mole-rat code, and Wilbur was the lone mole rat who enjoyed getting dressed. Consequently Wilbur felt alienated, and his clothing store was a disaster. When the patriarch mole rat—naked by custom—was consulted on the issue of clothing, he realized that it was an issue of individual choice and should not be a

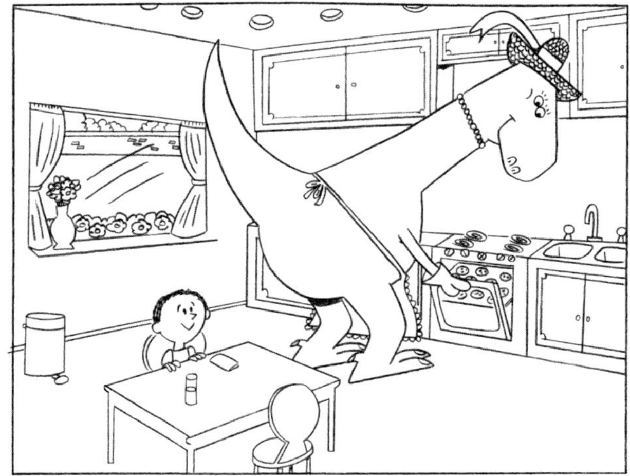

Hooray For Amanda & Her Alligator!, JAN 13, 2010, Ink

Edwina the Dinosaur Who Didn't Know She Was Extinct, ca. 2005, Black colored pencil

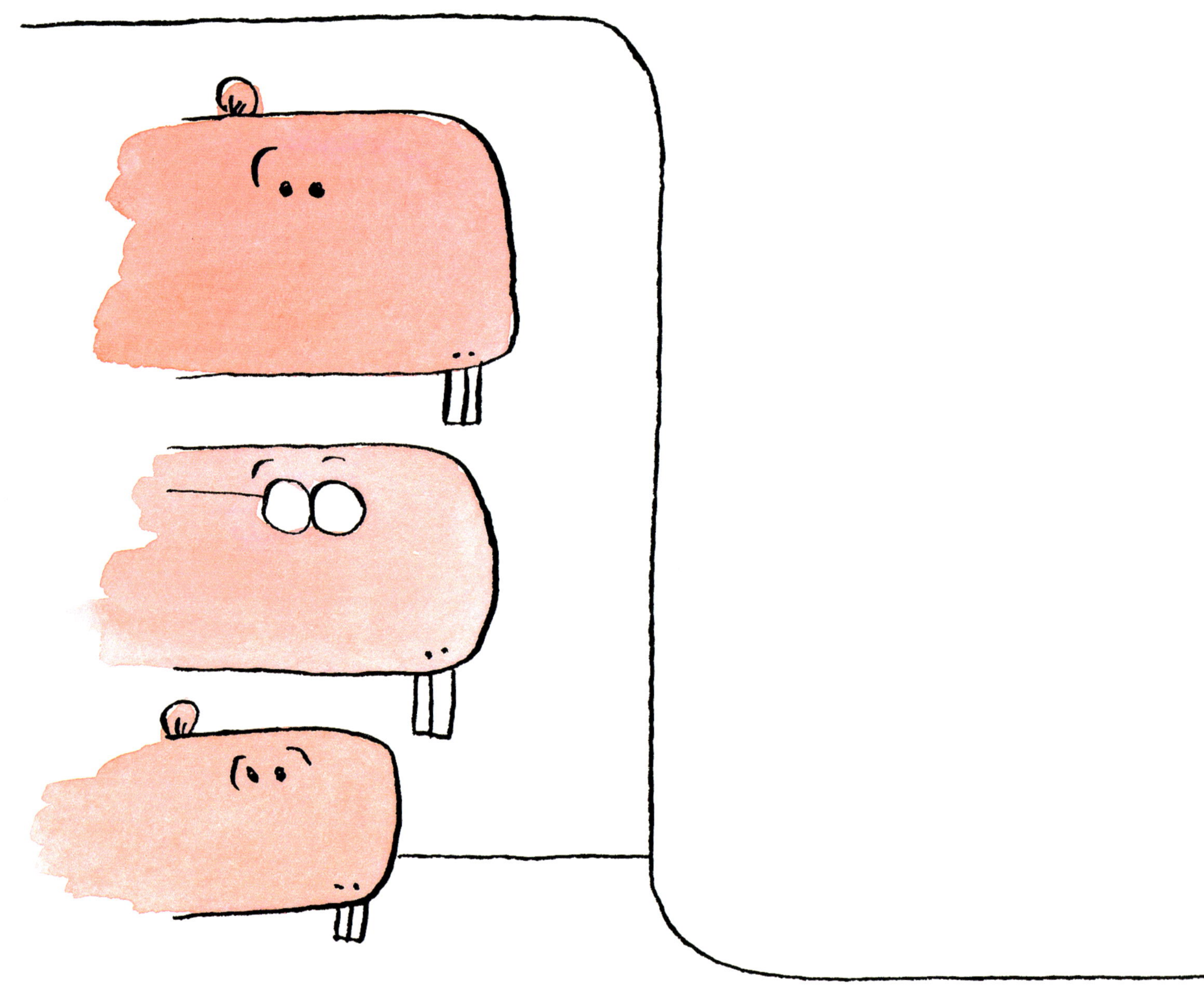

Naked Mole Rat Gets Dressed, NOV 25, 2007, Ink and watercolor

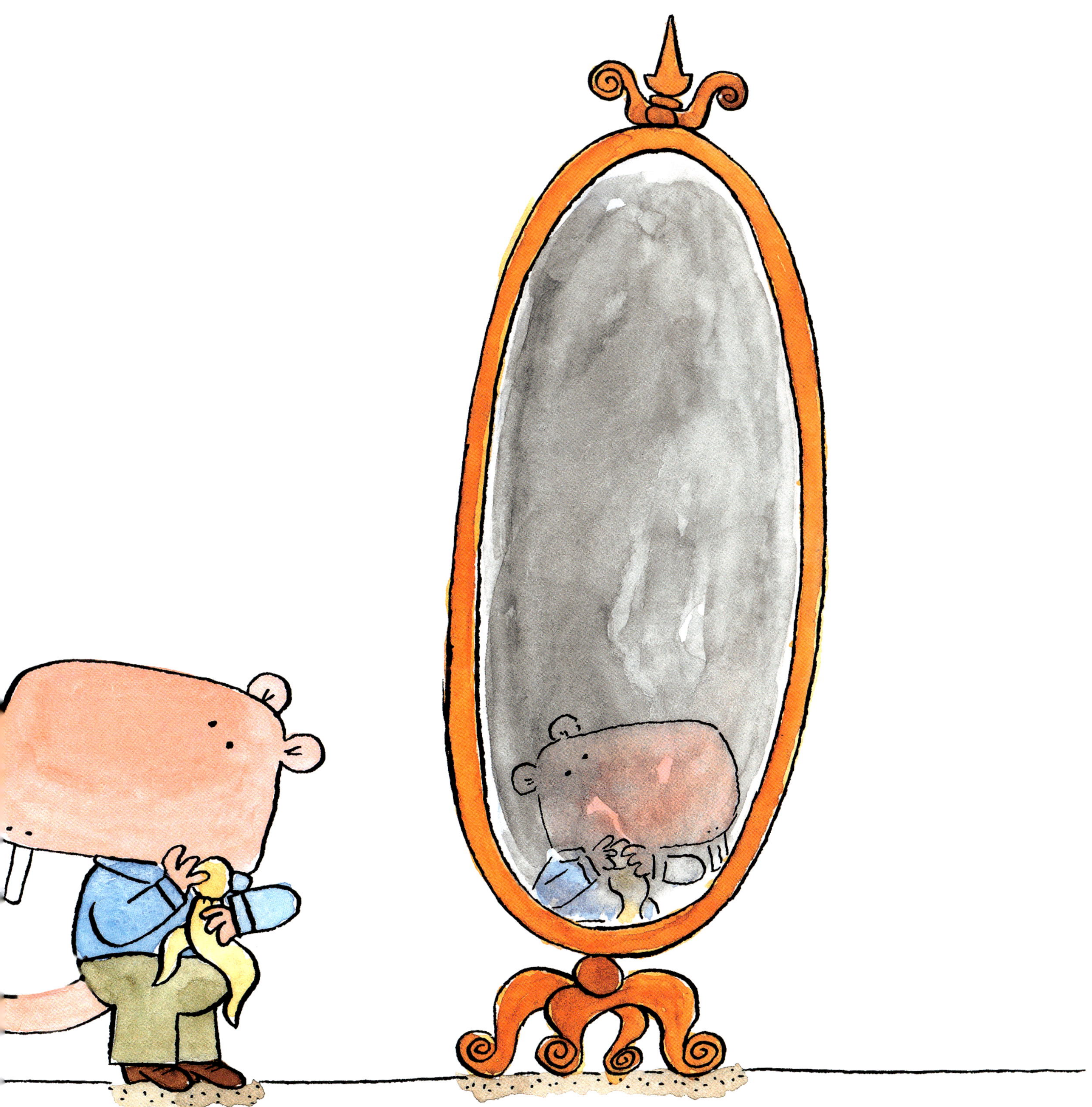

limiting determinant to conventional naked-mole-ratdom. The watercolors that form this book reveal the artist's delicacy of touch and his ongoing ability to convey a host of expressions and feelings with an economy of means. And its creation was all the more special since Willems was able to draw the characters using one of Charles Schulz's nibs.

One of Willems's most recent offerings, *Goldilocks and the Three Dinosaurs*, constitutes a deliciously absurd retelling of the classic story involving possible entrapment, definitely chocolate pudding, presumed relief for one irresponsible little girl, and disappointment for three conniving dinosaurs. Willems sets the tone of the book with his end sheets that suggest through the crossing out of myriad titles an extensive search for the best adversary, ranging from clams and eels to mastodons and orthodontists. The art is quintessential Willems with the by-now signature emphasis on visually lucid two-dimensional elements. Each page is filled with humorous details that the young reader (and the old reader for that matter) will delight in decoding. The book and its art underscore the point that ten years into making books for children, Willems has not lost an iota of originality or energy.

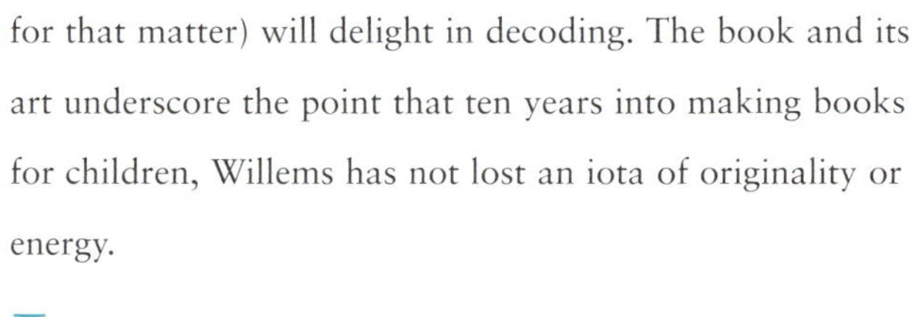

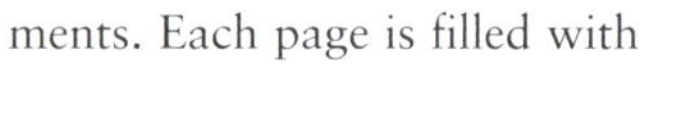

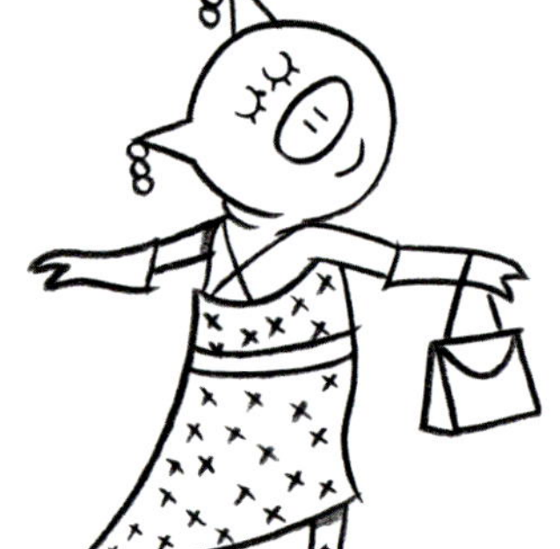

It is entirely fitting that the largest number of books Willems has published is devoted to helping and motivating the young child to learn to read. To this end he has taken another page from the Seussian playbook in creating lively texts accompanied by appealing and witty art that draw great sustenance from the well of silliness. Willems's trademark economy of means—whether in the text or in the image—inspires children to persevere in their quest for a fluent literacy. And he creates memorable characters in the process.

Laurel and Hardy, Abbott and Costello, Ethel and Lucy, Oscar and Felix, Bert and Ernie, Frog and Toad, George and Martha are all unforgettable duos who reside in the vaunted Pantheon of comedy. In their time, they have made audiences young and old laugh with their foibles and frailties. And so it is for Willems's Elephant and Piggie, who have graced us with more than nineteen books. The story lines—whether overcoming sadness, being invited to a party, balancing hippos on one's trunk, starring in a book, or

I Am Invited to a Party!, OCT 09, 2006, Charcoal pencil

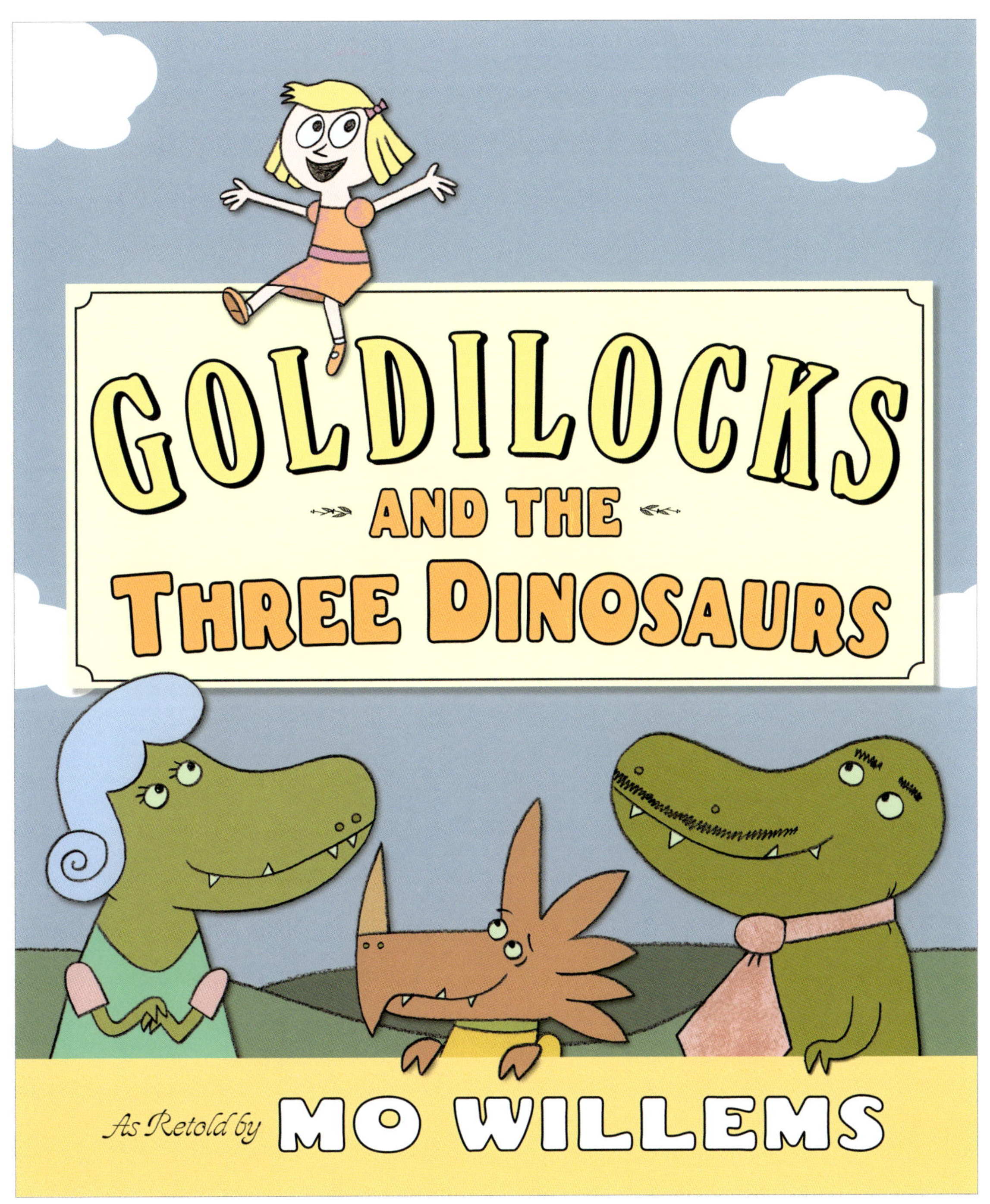

Published cover for *Goldilocks and the Three Dinosaurs*, 2012, Digital print

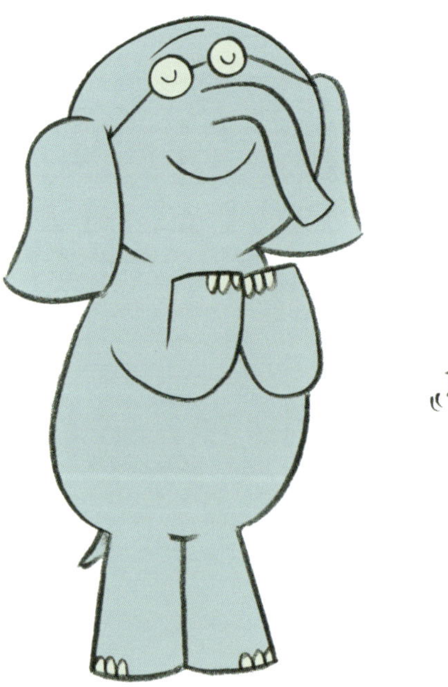

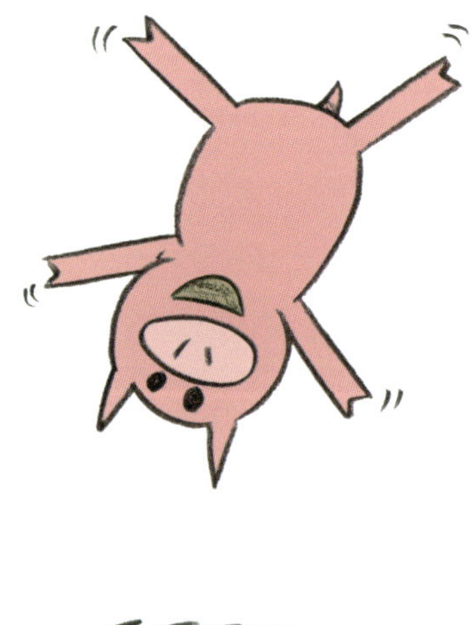

going for a drive—invariably build to a climax of high drama and emotional fervor. Just as invariably, the stories end with happy resolutions carrying a message of the value of loyalty in order for friendship to endure.

Willems, true to form, doesn't overwhelm the reader with text, and dialogue gains clarity by its inclusion in color-coded balloons. The art is equally understated, infatuating readers with superbly rendered gestures and facial expressions. The artist never ceases to reaffirm his astonishing ability to capture the deepest of human feelings with the subtlest shift in facial attributes (the eyes, eyebrows, or mouth) and body language (the slump of shoulders or the position of arms and legs). These books possess an almost pantomime quality—Elephant and Piggie meet Marcel Marceau—in the way the characters disport themselves across the pages. It is that visual and verbal reticence that leaves so much to the reader's imagination, so central to Willems's objective.

Published illustration for *Are You Ready to Play Outside?*, 2008, Digital print

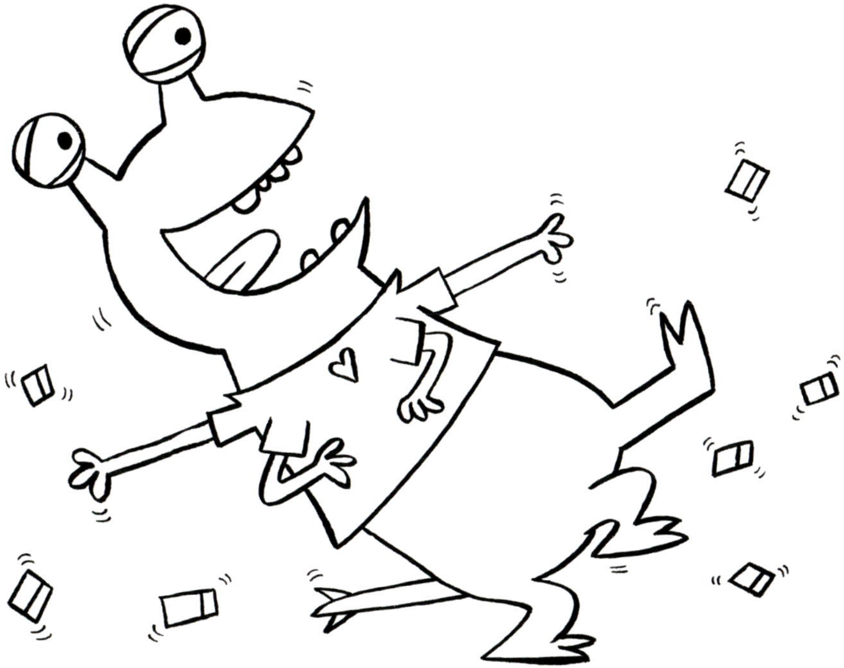

Willems's most recent series featuring Cat the Cat is geared to the nascent reader, where repetition assists in word recognition. Fortunately, we have come a long way from Dick and Jane, and Willems facilitates the reader's charge with bold and dynamic graphics, uncluttered settings, and an irrepressible sense of humor. Who would have thought "Blarggie! Blarggie!" could enter the literary lexicon? A ludicrous monster and a nonsensical word provide a compelling portal for the aspiring reader. The implied message that you can make friends with something or someone different is equally important. All of the books in the series make the task at hand mirthful and meaningful, and all of them carry subtle and not-so-subtle messages of caring for others and caring for oneself.

In ten years of creating books for children, Mo Willems has produced a substantial body of work that consistently meets the highest standards and exudes the dedication and finesse of the most accomplished of craftsmen. And this is how he likes to be considered; he eschews what for him is the high falutin' moniker of "artist." Yet one cannot deny the profound artistry of his work. Happily, he loves marrying the silly with the serious, and we are all the better for it.

Cat the Cat Who is That?, JUL 06, 2008, Ink brush

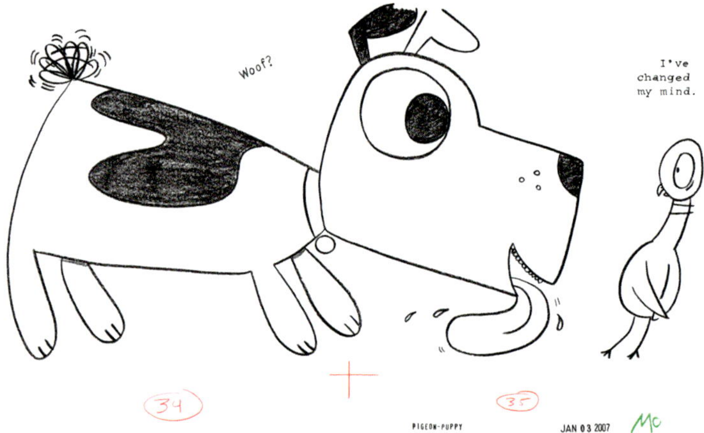

ILLUSTRATIONS

Unless otherwise noted, all works in this exhibition are by Mo Willems (American, b.1968), are lent by the artist, and are created on paper. All dates for published work relating to books are the date of publication. The dates for preliminary works are date specific.

Front cover: Final version for ***"Noooooooooooooooooooooooooooo!"*** DEC 08 2010, Aquarelle pencil
Back cover: ***Let's Go For a Drive!***, 2012, Digital print
Back cover flap: ***Don't Let the Pigeon Drive the Bus!***, 2003, Digital print
Page 1: ***KNUFFLE BUNNY, A Cautionary Tale***, 8/23/03, Ink
Pages 2–3: ***Leonardo the Terrible Monster***, 2005, Digital print

CHECKLIST

An asterisk denotes the work is illustrated.

Saul Steinberg (American, born in Romania, 1914-1999)
Arch, ca. 1950
Pen and Ink

Charles Schulz (American, 1922-2000)
*"April 1 Peanuts with Good 'ol' Charlie Brown," April 1, 1953
Pen and Ink
Reproduced with permission of Peanuts Worldwide LLC

Ronald Searle (British, 1920-2011)
Fellow with slots machine, Las Vegas, n.d.
Pen and Ink

Jean-Jacques Sempé (French, b. 1932)
Art Lovers, n.d.
Pen and Ink

William Steig (American, 1907-2003)
Late Night for Both, May 11, 1956
Collier's Weekly, Vol. 137 [May 11, 1956]
Pen and Ink

Fiep Westendorp (Dutch, 1916-2004)
*"Olifanten in het circus ("Elephants in the circus")," ca. 1965
Digital print
©Fiep Amsterdam bv; Fiep Westendorp Illustrations

Mo Willems (American, b. 1968)
*Concept Drawing for *Suzy Kabloozie sitting on a couch*, 1994
© 1994 by Sesame Street
Ink and cel paint on acetate

The Pigeon Books

Don't Let the Pigeon Drive the Bus! [New York: Hyperion Books for Children, 2003]

Curious Pictures presents: Don't Let the Pigeon Drive the Bus!: a mo willems sketchbook, 1998
Printed booklet

The Pigeon Wants a Puppy!, JAN 03, 2007, Aquarelle pencil

Pitch copy of *Don't Let the Pigeon Drive the Bus!!!*, 2003
Photocopy and crayon

Final version for cover of *Don't Let the Pigeon Drive the Bus!*, 3/14/02
Aquarelle pencil

*Published cover for *Don't Let the Pigeon Drive the Bus!*, 2003
Digital print
Reproduced with permission of Hyperion Books for Children
©2003 by Mo Willems

Final version for "Hey, I've got an idea. Let's play 'Drive the Bus'!," 3/13/02
Aquarelle pencil

*Preliminary sketch for "I'll be your best friend! / How 'bout I give you five bucks? / No fair! / I bet your mom would let me," 1/31/02
Graphite, red pencil, printed and pasted text
© 2003 by Mo Willems

*Published illustration for "I'll be your best friend! / How 'bout I give you five bucks? / No fair! / I bet your mom would let me," 2003
Digital print
Reproduced with permission of Hyperion Books for Children
© 2003 by Mo Willems

Final version for "LET ME DRIVE THE BUS!!!," ca. 2002
Aquarelle pencil

*Published illustration for "LET ME DRIVE THE BUS!!!," 2003
Digital print
Reproduced with permission of Hyperion Books for Children
© 2003 by Mo Willems

Final version for "downcast Pigeon," 2003
Aquarelle pencil

The Pigeon Finds a Hot Dog! [New York: Hyperion Books for Children, 2004]

*Final version for "Is that a hot dog?," 3/19/03
Aquarelle pencil
© 2004 by Mo Willems

Published illustration for "Is that a hot dog?," 2004
Digital print

Final version for "Hmmm . . . needs mustard," 3/19/03
Aquarelle pencil

Don't Let the Pigeon Stay Up Late! [New York: Hyperion Books for Children, 2006]

Final version for "OKAY, THAT WAS NOT A YAWN!," 1/03/05
Aquarelle pencil

*Final version for "You haven't heard—yawn—the—Yaaaawn—last of me!," 1/03/05
Aquarelle pencil
© 2006 by Mo Willems

The Pigeon Wants a Puppy! [New York: Hyperion Books for Children, 2008]

Work flow chart for *The Pigeon Wants a Puppy*, NOV 10 2006-JAN 04 2007
Mixed media

*Final version for "A PUPPY!," JAN 02 2007
Aquarelle pencil
© 2008 by Mo Willems

Preliminary sketch for "You don't want me to be happy, do you?" NOV 21 2006
Blue pencil and pasted text

*Final version for "I've changed my mind" JAN 03 2007
Aquarelle pencil
© 2008 by Mo Willems

The Duckling Gets a Cookie!? [New York: Hyperion Books for Children, 2012]

*Final version of cover for *The Duckling Gets a Cookie!?*, DEC 08 2010
Aquarelle pencil
© 2012 by Mo Willems

*Published cover for *The Duckling Gets a Cookie!?*, 2012
Digital print
Reproduced with permission of Hyperion Books for Children
© 2012 by Mo Willems

Final version for "So, you get a cookie with nuts, just by asking!?"/"Politely . . . ," DEC 08 2010
Aquarelle pencil

*Final version for "Noooooooooooooooooooooooooooo!" DEC 08 2010
Aquarelle pencil
© 2012 by Mo Willems

The Knuffle Bunny Books

KNUFFLE BUNNY, A Cautionary Tale [New York: Hyperion Books for Children, 2004]

Dummy for *Knuffle Bear*, 6/03
Red and blue colored pencil, graphite on printed grid

Work chart for *KNUFFLE BUNNY, A Cautionary Tale*, 7/03 – 1/04
Graphite, colored pencils, and Ink

Final version for Title page/"And those were the first words Trixie ever said," 8/17/03
Ink

*Published illustration for Title Page/"And those were the first words Trixie ever said," 2004
Digital print
Reproduced with permission of Hyperion Books for Children
© 2004 by Mo Willems

Preliminary sketch for "As soon as Trixie's mommy opened the door, she asked, 'Where's Knuffle Bunny?'" ca. 2003
Blue and red colored pencil

*Final version for "As soon as Trixie's mommy opened the door, she asked, 'Where's Knuffle Bunny?'," 8/23/03
Ink
© 2004 by Mo Willems

*Published illustration for "As soon as Trixie's mommy opened the door, she asked, 'Where's Knuffle Bunny?'," 2004
Digital print
Reproduced with permission of Hyperion Books for Children
© 2004 by Mo Willems

Final version for "Trixie helped her daddy put the laundry into the machine," 8/31/03
Ink

Final version for "She even got to put money into the machine," 8/31/03
Ink

Final version for "KNUFFLE BUNNY!!!" 2004
Ink
Published illustration for "KNUFFLE BUNNY!!!," 2004
Digital print

Preliminary sketch for "Trixie bawled. She went boneless," ca. 2003
Black and blue colored pencil
Private Collection

Preliminary sketch for "The whole family ran down the block," ca. 2003
Black colored pencil
Private Collection

Preliminary sketch for "[They zoomed past the school,] and into the Laundromat," ca. 2003
Black and blue colored pencil
Private Collection

KNUFFLE BUNNY TOO, A Case of Mistaken Identity [New York: Hyperion Books for Children, 2007]

*Workflow Chart for *KNUFFLE BUNNY TOO, A Case of Mistaken Identity*, ca. 2006
Mixed media
© 2007 by Mo Willems

Preliminary sketch for Title Page/"And that's how Trixie found her first* best friend (*Knuffle Bunny excepted, of course.),"
JUN 28 2006
Blue and red colored pencil

Final version for Title Page/"And that's how Trixie found her first* best friend (*Knuffle Bunny excepted, of course.)," JUL 3 2006
Ink

Final version for "The morning did not go well" JUL 14 2006
Ink

Final version for "'We have your bunny,' said a man's voice on the other end," JUN 30 2006
Ink

KNUFFLE BUNNY FREE, An Unexpected Diversion [New York: Balzer + Bray, an imprint of HarperCollins Publishers, 2010]

Workflow Chart for *KNUFFLE BUNNY FREE, An Unexpected Diversion*, APR 9 – AUG 16 2009
Graphite, colored pencils, and ink

*Preliminary sketch for "Watching Knuffle Bunny go through the big machine," JUN 05 2009
Blue and red colored pencil
© 2010 by Mo Willems

*Final version for "Watching Knuffle Bunny go through the big machine," JUL 06 2009
Ink
© 2010 by Mo Willems

*Published illustration for "Watching Knuffle Bunny go through the big machine," 2010
Digital print
Reproduced with permission of HarperCollins Publishers
© 2010 by Mo Willems

Preliminary sketch for "'KNUFFLE BUNNY!!!' Trixie was so happy to have Knuffle Bunny back in her arms" JUL 01 2009
Blue and red colored pencil

Final version for "Really' said Trixie. She was big enough," JUL 08 2009
Ink

Stand Alone Books

Time to Pee! [New York: Hyperion Books for Children, 2003]

Variant preliminary sketch for title page, 10/24/02
Graphite, blue and red colored pencil, and ink

*Final version for "that funny feeling," 8/23/02
Ink
© 2003 by Mo Willems

*Final version for "Boys can stand," 8/26/02
Ink
© 2003 by Mo Willems

Final version for "Girls should sit," 2002
Ink

Time to Say Please! [New York: Hyperion Books for Children, 2005]

Final version for "When you want a turn," 1/31/04
Ink

Unpublished drawing for *Time to Say Please!*, 12/2/03
Ink

Leonardo the Terrible Monster [New York: Hyperion Books for Children, 2005]

Final version for upper portion of "Leonardo tried very hard to be scary. But...," 7/7/04
Ink

*Final version for lower portion of "Leonardo tried very hard to be scary. But...," 7/7/04
Ink
© 2005 by Mo Willems

*Preliminary sketch for "Leonardo researched until he found the perfect candidate," 7/6/04
Graphite and blue pencil
© 2005 by Mo Willems

*Published illustration of "Leonardo researched until he found the perfect candidate," 2005
Digital print
Reproduced with permission of Hyperion Books for Children
© 2005 by Mo Willems

Preliminary sketch for "And the monster gave it all he had" 7/15/04
Ink

Edwina The Dinosaur Who Didn't Know She Was Extinct [New York: Hyperion Books for Children, 2006]

Final version for "Everybody loved Edwina . . . except Reginald Von Hoobie-Doobie," ca. 2005
Black colored pencil

*Final version for *Edwina baking cookies*, ca. 2005
Black colored pencil
© 2006 by Mo Willems

Naked Mole Rat Gets Dressed [New York: Hyperion Books for Children, 2009]

*Final version for "'Hello'," NOV 25 2007
Ink and watercolor
© 2007 by Mo Willems

Final version for "fancy," NOV 26 2007
Ink and watercolor

Final version for "or cool," NOV 28 2007
Ink and watercolor

Hooray for Amanda & Her Alligator! [New York: Balzer + Bray, an imprint of HarperCollins Publishers, 2011]

Final version for "So he gave it to himself," JAN 12 2010
Ink

*Final version for "Amanda was reading her new library book You Can Make It Yourself: Jet Packs! When she noticed her alligator chewing on her head," JAN 13 2010
Ink

Goldilocks and the Three Dinosaurs [New York: Balzer + Bray, an imprint of HarperCollins Publishers, 2012]

*Published cover illustration for *Goldilocks and the Three Dinosaurs*, 2012
Digital print
Used by permission of HarperCollins Publishers

*Final version for "Suddenly — and completely coincidentally — the three Dinosaurs rushed through the front door," MAY 20 2011
Ink

*Published illustration for "Suddenly — and completely coincidentally — the three Dinosaurs rushed through the front door," 2012
Digital print
Used by permission of HarperCollins Publishers

Early Readers

Elephant and Piggie

My Friend is Sad (an ELEPHANT & PIGGIE book) [New York: Hyperion Books for Children, 2007]

Final Version for "A funny, funny clown!," JAN 17 2006
Charcoal pencil

*Final version for *Elephant and Piggie leaning against each other, smiling*, JAN 17 2006
Charcoal pencil

I Am Invited to a Party! (an ELEPHANT & PIGGIE book) [New York: Hyperion Books for Children, 2007]

*Final version for "Very fancy," OCT 09 2006
Charcoal pencil

Final version for "You do know parties!/Party! Party! Party!," OCT 11 2006
Charcoal pencil

Are You Ready to Play Outside? (an ELEPHANT & PIGGIE book) [New York: Hyperion Books for Children, 2008]

Final version for "We are going to jump!," JUL 05 2007
Charcoal pencil

*Published illustration for "We are going to jump!," 2008
Digital print
Reproduced with permission of Hyperion Books for Children

Can I Play Too? (an ELEPHANT & PIGGIE book) [New York: Hyperion Books for Children, 2010]

Final version for "No! We *do* want to play catch with you. But . . .," NOV 25 2008
Charcoal pencil

Final version for "Bonk! Bonk! Bonk!," NOV 18 2008
Charcoal pencil

We Are in a Book! (an ELEPHANT & PIGGIE book) [New York: Hyperion Books for Children, 2010]

Draft 1 for *We Are in a Book!*, APR 8-23 2009
Graphite, blue and red colored pencil

Final version for "A reader is reading us!," MAY 06 2009
Charcoal pencil

Final version for "WE ARE BEING READ! WE ARE BEING READ!," APRIL 28 2009
Charcoal pencil

Final version for "The Reader said . . . Hee! Hee! Hee! Hee! Hee!," MAY 3 2009
Charcoal pencil

Final version for "This book is going *too* fast!," APRIL 30 2009
Charcoal pencil

I Broke My Trunk! (an ELEPHANT & PIGGIE book) [New York: Hyperion Books for Children, 2011]

Final version for *Balancing two hippos, one rhino, and a piano*, SEP 06 2009
Charcoal pencil

Final version for "You broke your trunk running to tell me your story?,"
SEP 07 2009
Charcoal pencil

Let's Go for a Drive! (an ELEPHANT & PIGGIE book) [New York: Hyperion books for Children, 2012]

Preliminary sketch for "'We need bags!' I have bags!',"
SEP 08 2011
Blue colored pencil

Final version for "'We need bags!' I have bags!'," SEP 29 2011
Charcoal pencil

*Published illustration for "We need bags..." 2012
Digital print
Reproduced with permission of Hyperion Books for Children
© 2012 by Mo Willems
(Catalogue only)

Final version for "There will be a lot of *driving* on our drive!,"
OCT 2011
Charcoal pencil

Cat the Cat

Cat the Cat Who is That? [New York: Balzer + Bray, an imprint of HarperCollins Publishers, 2010]

Final version for "It's Duck the duck," JUL 05 2008
Ink brush

*Final version for "Blarggie! Blarggie!," JUL 06 2008
Ink brush
© 2010 by Mo Willems

Final version for "It's a NEW friend! Blarggie! Blarggie!"
JUL 04 2008
Ink brush

Published illustration for "It's a NEW friend! Blarggie! Blarggie!,"
2010
Digital print

Let's Say HI to Friends Who FLY! [New York: Balzer + Bray, an imprint of HarperCollins Publishers, 2010]

Final version for "ZOOM!," SEP 23 2008
Ink brush

Final version for *Rhino in plane*, SEP 23 2008
Ink brush

Time to Sleep, Sheep the Sheep! [New York: Balzer + Bray, an imprint of HarperCollins Publishers, 2010]

Preliminary sketch for "'Time to sleep, Horse the Horse!'," FEB 25 2009
Blue and red colored pencil

Final version for "'Time to sleep, Horse the Horse!'," MAR 1 2009
Ink brush

What's Your Sound, Hound the Hound? [New York: Balzer + Bray, an imprint of HarperCollins Publishers, 2010]

Final version for "What's your sound, Cow the Cow?," FEB 13 2009
Ink brush

Final version for *Cow standing by fridge*, FEB 12 2009

What's Your Sound, Hound the Hound? [New York: Balzer + Bray, an imprint of HarperCollins Publishers, 2010]
Ink brush

Independent Art

Pigeon Sculpture, 2011
Wire and wood

Elephant Sculpture, 2000
Wire

"The Lady Has Arrived," 2007
Ink and crayon on envelope

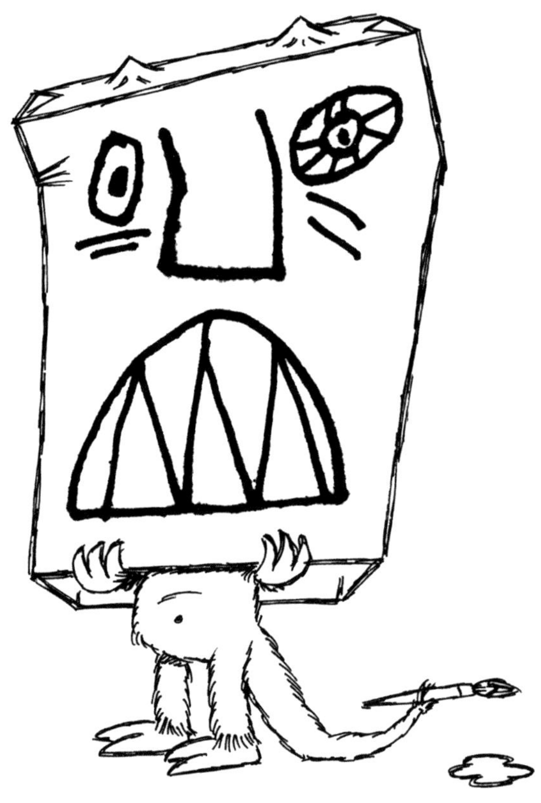

Published by The Eric Carle Museum of Picture Book Art

ISBN 978-1-59288-030-0
Printed in Italy

First Edition

Leonardo the Terrible Monster, 7/7/04, Ink